World War II History

World War II History

Angus Rutherford

CONTENTS

World War II History

True Stories of Survival From the Blitz of London

Angus Rutherford

Introduction

The Blitz was a heavy and frequent bombing attack on the city of London and other cities during World War II. The Nazi German bombing session against the United Kingdom happened in 1940 and 1941. It was a lighting war between Germany and the United Kingdom as the city of London was bombed night after night and day after day. After the surrender of France in June of 1940, Hitter passed a directive commanding the preparation and enactment (if possible) of Operation Sea Lion, which was the amphibious invasion of Great Britain. Seeing Britain's Royal Navy approaching from the surface with full control in the channel, Luftwaffe came to execute dominance of the skies over the battle zone.

On August 2, the commander of the German force, Hermann Goring, brought forward his Eagle Day directive mapping a strategy of attack. The plan mentioned a few major blows from the air to eliminate the British airpower from the way of invasion (Britannica, 2018). The Luftwaffe hoped that a victory in this war would bring Britain to invasion and occupation. However, RAF's victory did not open this possibility and led to the survival of Britain and destruction of the Third Reich. The possibility of the victory of the Royal Force was significantly impacted by the lack of planning from the Germans. They first attempted to bring a blockade by destroying port and shipping facilities, the other times they directly attacked the Royal Army's ground installations. Sometimes their attacks were directed toward aircraft factories and the other times they were trying to misdirect Fighter Command in the air.

On the other hand, the British force was well prepared for the battle. They used their Chain Home early warning radar, RAF Spitfire, and other superior equipment to fight against the Germans. They directed Fighter Command the right way and used their superlative fighter against German bombers and Bf 109. Nevertheless, the bigger numbers brought the Germans close to victory in late August 1940 (Britannica,

2018). More than 600 Luftwaffe aircraft were destroyed. Although RAF had lost not even half their numbers, the experienced pilots and British fighters were claimed at a big rate. Instead of taking the right advantage of this situation, Hitler switched his strategy all of a sudden. The civilian areas of London were bombed in late August, which was claimed to be an accident. Following this, the British counterattacked Germany by launching a bombing raid on Berlin on August 25. The Commander of the German Raid had claimed that such an attack was not possible due to the forbidden air defense network of the city. The event provoked Hitler to command the attacks by the Luftwaffe to shift from RAF areas to London and other cities (Britannica, 2018). On September 7, 1940, Nazi Reichsmarschall Hermann Goring, from his vantage spot in Normandy, directed his binoculars towards the English coast (*The Cruel Cost of the Blitz*, 2017). On a historic day amid the Second World War, about one thousand German bomber and fighter aircraft left their camps to move towards London, the English capital to begin their bombing campaign (*The Cruel Cost of the Blitz*, 2017). This was the fateful day that gave a start to the eight months of the bombing campaign. Luftwaffe dropped bombs on London and other planned cities throughout Britain (Britannica, 2018). The man who authorized this campaign, then German chancellor- Adolf Hitler, hoped that these consecutive bomb attacks on Britain would soon bring Germany to overpower. The same day, Goring had broadcasted a confident statement on the radio: "This is a historic hour, in which for the first time the German Luftwaffe has struck at the heart of the enemy" (*The Cruel Cost of the Blitz*, 2017).

This attack was far from the near-wars that happened between Germany and Britain the previous October. Although the September raids were not the first attack that Britain suffered, this was a massive bombardment and Britain had never seen anything close to it before. Through the Blitz, Germans assumed that Hitler's plan to take over Britain was failing. After the war with France, Britain was the power that stood in the way of Germany's victory (*The Cruel Cost of the Blitz*, 2017).

However, despite the delivery of Anderson air-raid shelters, the evacuation of residents, and the founding of the Air Raid Precautions organization, there was a huge loss of life due to the air attacks. Despite official attempts, many individuals were denied proper shelters, and therefore subterranean options, mainly tube stations were hijacked for this purpose (*The Cruel Cost of the Blitz*, 2017). The Blitz's primary phase came to a conclusion in May 1941. The Luftwaffe was taking more casualties as a result of advanced British air defenses, which were supported by radar advancements. Probably, Germany needed resources diverted to the east in preparation for its impending invasion of the Soviet Union.

The British government had forewarned of airstrikes on its population centers, and it had anticipated terrible losses. During the Spanish Civil War, a Luftwaffe terror bombing of the city of Guernica (April 26, 1937) had taken the lives of hundreds of people and damaged most of the city. The British government launched a huge evacuation plan on September 1, 1939, the day World War II started with Germany's invasion of Poland. An estimated one and a half million citizens, the vast majority of whom were children, were evacuated from densely populated metropolitan areas to nearby rural regions that were considered safe (Britannica, 2018). The massive evacuation, named Operation Pied Piper, was the greatest internal movement in British history.

Planning for bomb-proofing London and housing for those who got lost by the attacks was swiftly put into action by the authorities. Local governments were also given money to build public air-raid shelters by the federal government. The Department of Air Raid Precaution headed up by Sir John Anderson, distributed over 2 million Anderson shelters to the public. These corrugated steel shelters were made to be buried in the ground and then filled with soil (Britannica, 2018). As a result of the cold and damp conditions, Anderson shelters were not suitable for long-term occupancy. In the absence of basements, the A.R.P. developed the Morrison shelter (named for Home Secretary Herbert Stanley Morrison) as a feasible alternative to the Anderson shelter during World War II. Shelters for two adults and two small children, such as this one, were designed to be set up indoors and serve as a safe haven in case of a building collapse.

At the end of the Battle of Britain in 1940, the Germans launched a series of bombing raids on commercial targets, cities, and towns, including London. After losing the War of Britain in September 1940, the Luftwaffe was instructed to strike London in an attempt to pull RAF Fighter Command into a war of destruction. The new strategy was implemented on September 6, 1940 by Adolf Hitler and Reichsmarschall Hermann Göring, the head of the Luftwaffe. The Luftwaffe relentlessly bombarded London for 56 consecutive days and nights beginning on September 7, 1940. On September 15, a large-scale attack was launched in London in broad daylight.

After October 1940, the Blitz turned into a night bombing campaign as the Luftwaffe drastically limited daytime operations in favor of night strike to dodge attacks from the RAF. During the Liverpool Blitz, the Luftwaffe bombed a major port on Liverpool's Atlantic coast. The Hull Blitz struck the North Sea port of Hull, which bombers used as a fallback if they couldn't find their intended targets. They also bombed the port cities of Bristol, Portsmouth, Swansea Cardiff, Southampton, Plymouth, Belfast, and Glasgow and even the industrial centers of Birmingham, Coventry, Sheffield, and Manchester. Wartime Luftwaffe bombing took the lives of more than 40,000 people, with about half of those deaths occurring in Berlin, where over a million homes were severely damaged.

However, this was the last such attack until January of 1943, when the war ended.

Even though London took the brunt of the Blitz's attacks, the Blitz was an all-out invasion of the United Kingdom. Only a few locations escaped the wrath of the airstrikes. A strong airstrike might have a disastrous effect on small, densely populated communities. Major commercial cities and provincial hubs began to be attacked in the middle of November 1940. Another series of attacks, this time diverted towards the ports, started in early 1941. June brought some pause from the heavy bombardment of Russia and the Mediterranean by the Luftwaffe at that time.

Over the winter of 1940–1941, the Luftwaffe's tactics grew more aimless. Rather than strategy, disagreements among OKL employees focused more on methods. This strategy was doomed to failure before it had even begun. It was becoming more difficult to have a strategic impact because of the limits of weapons technology and the speed of British responses. Coal was an essential fuel for many industrial economies during the Second World War; delaying train traffic and interfering with shipping and imports had a favorable effect.

The use of delayed-action bombs, which were first quite successful, progressively lost their effectiveness due to their failure to explode. To avoid a complete assault on its manufacturing facilities, the British prepared for the shift in strategies by dispersing its industrial sites. To keep the war economy going, regional commissioners were granted plenipotentiary powers to reestablish communications and organize the transfer of supplies. Luftwaffe's strategy was to continue attacking London, mostly at night, to disrupt production in the West Midlands' large industrial weapons manufacturers, and to interrupt factories and plants during the day with fighter-bombers.

Kesselring, commanding Luftflotte 2, was instructed to fly 50 attacks a night against London and to bomb the eastern ports during the daytime hours. As commander of Luftflotte 3, Sperrle was charged with launching 250 missions every night, 100 of which were to target the West Midlands. Tenth Air Corps (Fliegerkorps X) was assigned to conduct Seeschlange, a mining operation targeting ships. It also played an active role in the bombardment of Britain. It had thrown 3,984 mines, one-third of the total on April 19/20, 1941. It was anticipated in Britain that the mines might devastate whole cities, but some came into British hands unexploded and allowed countermeasures to be built that crippled the German anti-shipping operation.

Approximately 13,000 short tons of high explosives and approximately one million explosives had been dropped on London by mid-November 1940 when the Germans modified their strategy. No significant raids were conducted outside the city, although single aircraft were engaged in the broad destructive activity and quite powerful diversionary strikes on Coventry, Birmingham, and Liverpool. Transport infrastructure in London had been severely damaged, including the ports and rail links. At one point, between 5,000 and 6,000 carriages were stranded due to the effects of delayed-action bombs on Great Britain's railways in September.

Many commuters had to make unusual routes through back streets or check anxiously at the list of lines blocked at their local station each morning, but they still made it to work. The monitors sent out by the Ministry of Home Security were unable to find any evidence of a moral breakdown despite the damage to lives and property. In September and October alone, more than 13,000 people were killed and almost 20,000 were wounded, yet the death toll was far lower than projected. Churchill gave credit to the shelters in the latter part of 1940. Hitler, on the other hand, was enraged and mystified that the continuous bombing of Britain had failed to destroy the determination and spirit of the British. He met his generals in Boulogne during Christmas 1940 and instructed them to immediately prepare for a huge attack on London that'd devastate the City's commercial and historic center around St Paul's Cathedral (London Walking Tours, n.d.).

Such an assault could only be successful under the following circumstances:

1. High explosives would cause water mains to burst in the City of London, therefore a low tide was necessary. As a last measure, the London Fire Brigade would have to turn to the River Thames for water.
2. Anti-aircraft weapons protected by low cloud cover at 5,000 feet.

As most office employees would be at home on a Sunday, there'd be no key holders available to open the doors of the buildings, making it an ideal day for a break-in. As a result, firefighters would be forced to enter the structures, which would have already been engulfed in flames from the incendiary bombs by that time. On Sunday, December 29, 1940, all of these factors came together, and Hitler called Hugo Sperrle (General Commander of Luftflotte 111) and ordered him to conduct a huge attack on London's financial district that night (London Walking Tours, n.d.).

1

The Happening

September 7, 1940, also known as the "Black Saturday," is the date that will go down as one of the darkest days in human history. It was the day when the Horror of The London Blitz started to rule over the people of Britain.

On September 7, 1940, many German bombers suddenly appeared over the blue skies of London to instill the terror of Nazi Germany on them. Roughly at 4:00 PM on that September day, hundreds of these bombers escorted by around 600 fighters blasted London until 6:00 PM. When the Britishers thought they could have a sigh of relief, the second group of bombers invaded to bomb the east end of London. This raid started two hours after the first one had finished. But this time, the German bombers, guided with fire assaults, bombed the region till 4:30 in the morning. That was the start of a deliberate strategy planned by Germany's Chancellor Adolf Hitler to subdue Great Britain. The bombing continued till the following May, wreaking havoc on London and other important cities of Great Britain.

Since the first day of the bombing, London saw an intense period of bombing and firing for the next 57 consecutive days. The people were terrified of the attackers as they could bomb their house at any given point, whether it was day or night. Residents sought shelters wherever they could find them. At one point, the underground stations sheltered well over 177,000 people during the night. In the worst incident, around 450 people got killed when the bombers bombed a school used as a raid shelter for the citizens (Salisbury, 2012). The Londoners and the world got introduced to the new weapon of terror in the arsenal of 20th-century conflicts. Finally, the Blitz ended on May 11, 1941, when Hitler withdrew the bombers from London because he needed them for the Russian invasion. But why did it start in the first place? It was the reply of the Nazis to the nighttime air raid carried out by the British on Berlin. If we go by the records, the main aim was to demoralize the population and get Britain to come to the Nazi's terms. This offense came to be known as the Blitz, which derived from the German word *blitzkrieg*, meaning "lightning war."

The Battle of Great Britain

Before we dive into the Blitz in detail, we need to look at the chain of events that led to the London Blitz. One of the major causes was "The Battle of Great Britain." In the spring of 1940, the Nazi armies made their way through the borders of the Netherlands and Belgium. It helped them reach the northern borders of France. The German forces quickly moved to the west and south, splitting the French and English armies into halves. This strategy helped them trap the British troops at Dunkirk, forcing their evacuation from continental Europe. The Nazis entered Paris on June 14 and forced France to surrender, which they finally did on June 22.

Britain: The Sole Enemy Across the English Channel

With France surrendering to the Nazis, Great Britain was in trouble as it was the sole enemy of Germany left across the English channel. The soldiers who got rescued from Dunkirk were down and exhausted; most of their heavy armaments lay deserted on the shores of France.

On July 16, 1940, Hitler issued a directive that permitted the execution of Operation Sea Lion (an amphibious invasion of Britain), if necessary. Britain had a strong Navy; hence it would have been challenging to invade them through the surface. On top of it, Britain's Royal Navy was specifically controlling the surface approaches on the channel and the North Sea. Hence, the responsibility was laid on the shoulders of the Luftwaffe to establish dominance over the skies of the battlefield.

A victory for the Luftwaffe in the battle of Britain would have led Great Britain into more significant trouble. Their loss would expose Britain to attacks and occupation by the Nazis. On the contrary, if the Royal Air Force (RAF) wins, it would block the possibilities of invasion. It will create the conditions necessary for Britain's survival.

The End of the Battle of Great Britain

The British armies were ready for the kind of war they now found themselves in. The only thing that was standing between Britain and defeat was the RAF. The Nazis heavily outnumbered the British troops as for every British soldier, there were four Nazi fighters. RAF fought bravely against the bombers who came to kill them. Although, the British's RAF did bend but did not break.

Due to the sheer difference between their armies, Germany was on the brink of victory in late August 1940. The Luftwaffe had lost over 600 planes during the battle, and the RAF had lost fewer than half that many. This battle was absorbing Britain's experienced pilots and fighters. Instead of using this to his advantage, Hitler changed his strategies. In August 1940, Germans dropped some bombs over the civilian areas of London. According to Nazis, this bombing apparently got done by an accident. Great Britain retaliated by launching a similar bombing raid on Berlin on August 24, 1940. This raid got Hitler so infuriated that he ordered the Luftwaffe to shift its attacks from RAF to London and other important cities (Britannica, 2018).

Preparations Before the Blitz

The British government had anticipated attacks on their population centers because of the history of Nazis. They had predicted that there would be a catastrophic number of casualties. If we go back in time, we will see the true terror of Nazi bombings. During the Spanish civil war, a Luftwaffe terror bombing attack happened on the Spanish city of Guernica, which killed hundreds of civilians and destroyed much of the town.

The Mass Internal Migration

The British government implemented a mass evacuation plan to save its population from the Nazi bombings. In just three days, some 1.5 million civilians, including an overwhelming number of children, were transported from the urban areas to the rural villages. These rural areas were thought to be much safer than the urban areas since Nazis would target the urban regions. This mass relocation, called the Operation Pied Piper, was the most extensive internal migration in British history.

Various authorities swiftly implemented plans to protect the Londoners from bombs. Plans got made so that shelters could be provided to those who lost their homes by the attacks. The national government did fund local municipalities. These funds helped local administrations to construct public air-raid shelters. Around two million Anderson shelters were distributed among many households by the Air Raid Precautions (ARP) department. Although the Anderson shelters provided good protection against the bomb fragments and debris, they were damp and cold. They were ill-suited for prolonged occupancy by the British population. Keeping this in mind, the ARP devised Morrison shelters that could get used as an alternative to Anderson shelters. Morrison ones could fit two adults and two small children in it.

Beginning of the Dark

"Behind the lines" conditions prevailed in Britain during the initial years of the Second World War. Despite blackouts, shelters, sandbags, mass evacuations, ARP wardens, and members of Home Guard drilling in the parks, life went usual for most parts. The winters of 1939–40 were severe, but the summer went pleasant for the Londoners. They would stroll in parks or work in their gardens during their leisure time. Many theaters and cinemas were opened during that period, even sporting events were held.

There were no sirens wailed in London despite one or two false alarms in the early days of the war. Then the day came—June 25, 1940. That day the first siren wailed in the streets of London. The first week of September abruptly shattered the relative calmness as the war came into London.

The Raids by Nazi Germany

The Blitz began at 4:00 PM in the afternoon of September 7, 1940. For the next two hours, 348 German bombers and 617 fighters hovered over the city of London, intending to destroy the city. Later on, the second wave of planes came, but this time, they were guided by the raging fires of the first wave. It was a prolonged wave as it lasted till the early morning of September 8, 1940. Within a few hours, the Blitz had killed over 430, and around 1,600 got injured.

The Luftwaffe continued to bomb London for the next 57 consecutive nights. Between Black Saturday and December 2, there was not a single day that went without at least one 'alert' signal. In worse-case scenarios, the Londoners listened to nine alert signals, that too on three separate occasions. The only days where the peace of London wasn't disrupted by an alarm or bomb were November 3 and 28. Although night raids were happening continuously, the Luftwaffe also carried out attacks during the daytime. The mass attacks during the day proved costly to them during the Battle of Britain, so they switched it with smaller parties that came over in successive waves.

The London Raids

The Raids on London primarily focused on the Dockland areas of the east end. The ports were legitimate targets for the Luftwaffe because of their trade facilities. Around 25,000 bombs were dropped on the Port of London alone. These bombings also decreased Britain's war production to a significant amount. Docklands was also a densely populated region that consisted of the working class of London. Hence, these raids killed a significant number of civilians and left many other people homeless. Charitable relief was opened for the people of London in September 1940. Many countries around the world donated. By October 28, the contributions were enough to cover the United Kingdom and Northern Ireland. By the middle of December 1940, the donations had reached 1.7 million euros. When adjusted for inflation, this amount would be roughly 100 million euros in 2022.

The Depressing Expansion

Nazis expanded their target regions in November 1940. Besides London, the heavily bombed cities were Liverpool and Birmingham. The other target regions were Southampton, Manchester, Sheffield, and Coventry. The bombing on the old Coventry was particularly destructive. On November 14, around 500 bombers invaded Conventry and wreaked havoc over the city. Over 550 casualties were recorded on that day. The destruction was so significant that the Germans came up with a new verb, "to coventrate," to describe this attack. By May, the bombing had reached all the major cities of Britain, including Plymouth, Bristol, Newcastle, etc (Britannica, 2018). The night raids continued in London in 1941, where January 10–11 saw devastating attacks. The Mansion House and The Bank of England merely survived the destruction due to the bomb landing directly between them, creating a gigantic crater. Another large-scale attack followed on March 19, where hundreds of houses, shops, hospitals, churches, and other public buildings were destroyed by the Luftwaffe.

A similar attack happened on April 16, which started at 9:00 PM and lasted till 5:00 AM in the morning. It gets believed that around 500 bombers flew around the area and dropped 450 tons of bombs across the city, causing mass destruction. The ending of the 8 month long Blitz happened on May 10–11, when more than 500 German planes dropped more than 700 tons of bombs. The casualties were significant as 1,500 were killed, and 11,000 houses were destroyed. The House of Commons, Westminster Abbey, and the British Museum were severely damaged by the bombs. The Temple was left in a dismantled state after this infuriating and most intense raid of the Blitz (Britannica, 2018).

Response

In response to the Blitz, the British government took various measures to disrupt the plans of German bombers. They enforced blackouts to make aiming more difficult for the night bombers. Streetlights, car headlights, Illuminati signals were kept off. People hung black curtains in their houses which prevented light from going outside. Whenever a raid was about to happen, air raid sirens were set off to warn the Londoners. During the initial periods of the Blitz, British gunners were unable to inflict any significant damage on the German bombers. But later, the radar guidance system was developed that helped increase the efficiency of both antiaircraft artillery and searchlights.

The most impressive measure that the British government took against the German bombers was the "barrage balloons." These were enormous oval-shaped unmanned balloons with stabilizing tail fins. They were installed in and around prominent target areas and worked as an airspace denial tool. They prevented many low-altitude bombers from reaching their targets at optimal altitude and angles for the attack. Germans had to fly higher to avoid these balloons, but they had to compromise with their aims. These balloons were anchored to the ground with the help of steel tethers that were strong enough to damage or destroy any German plane that entered British territory. More than 100 planes came in contact with the barrage balloons, and around two-thirds of them crashed or were forced to land on British soil.

Seeking Shelter in the Blitz

The government did predict that they would suffer through fatal deaths. The initial human cost was lower than the expectations, but the levels of destruction exceeded the anticipations of the government. No matter how extensive the preparations for the Blitz were, the early bombing campaign made it clear that they were inadequate.

People had to get into the surface shelters constructed by the local authorities. Although these shelters were fully occupied during the nights, only 9% of the Londoners used them. 27% of the population utilized private shelters, and the remaining spent their time on the duty of civil defense or remained in their homes.

The South Hallsville School Massacre

The South Hallsville School massacre happened on September 10 that ignited public anger. After the bombing started on September 7, many people were displaced to take refuge in the South Hallsville School. Those people were reassured that they would be transported to a safer place, but for some reason, the evacuation got delayed. And on September 10, the school was devoured by the German Bombers. The government then declared that 77 people had died, but many believed the deaths were much higher. It is estimated that around 600 men, women, and children were killed in the explosion of South Hallsville School.

This incident prompted the Londoners to look for safer shelters on their own, if necessary. Many people sought refuge in the underground tunnels or railway stations of the city. Although, many officials forbid this idea because they thought that people would be reluctant to continue their regular lives on the surface. Using the Tube system as shelter saved thousands of lives. The pictures of people huddling in the underground stations would become unforgettable memories of British life in World War II.

The Impact and Legacy of the London Blitz

The Blitz shattered the British government, its people, and its cities. In eight months, 43,000 civilians were devoured by the Luftwaffe fighters. This amount was nearly half the total civilian deaths that happened during the second world war in Britain. One in every six Londoners was homeless at some point during the Blitz. It is estimated that at least 1.1 million houses and flats were damaged and destroyed by the bombings. As mentioned earlier, the main motive of the Blitz was to break the morale of the British people, which would have helped them pressure their government to surrender. Although, in the end, this campaign proved to be a strategic mistake by Hitler and the Germans. 'Business as usual' was written with chalk on boarded-up shop windows. This exemplified the British determination to keep calm and carry on as best they could. The morale of the public did bend due to the vast destruction, but they did not give up.

The Blitz came out as a counterproductive move. It wasn't able to serve the military purpose of dominating the skies of Britain. Hitler's main motive was to get control of England, but his plan was devastated by the RAF. By mid-September, RAF had won the Battle of Britain, which postponed the English invasion indefinitely.

2

The War Expansion

According to German POWs, the British would never discover the Knickebein even though it was there in front of their eyes in June 1940. Dr. R. V. Jones, a technical adviser for the RAF Air Staff, was informed of the discussion and began an investigation that discovered that Luftwaffe Lorenz receivers were far more than oblivious assistance. Beam Approach Training Development Unit (BATDU) Avro Ansons equipped with a 30 MHz receiver were operated around the country in search of German beams (Nambi, 2021). The location of a beam was quickly narrowed down to Derby (which had been mentioned in Luftwaffe transmissions). Electrocautery devices seized from a nearby hospital were used in the initial jamming operations. British Electronic Counter Measures (ECM) units of the No. 80 RAF Wing, led by Wing Commander Edward Addison, carried out the counter-operations. Meaconing is the practice of re-transmitting radio navigation signals using masking beacons to produce false signals. By the time the Luftwaffe was ready to carry out large-scale bombing operations, confidence in the device had lagged due to the use of nine special transmitters that expanded the beams' pathways.

It was possible for the Luftwaffe forces to identify the signal's bearing with the use of two-letter Morse codes, which were followed by a long pause. There were different locations for the receiver and the transmitter in the meacon system. The receiver sent the German signal to the transmitter, which then repeated it. Taking this step did not automatically result in success. The greater signal from the meacon was picked up by the location sensor if the German bomber flew closer to its own beam than it did from the meacon. Only if the meacon were closer would make the reverse be true. Generally speaking, German bombers were able to reach their objectives without any trouble. While it would be months before an effective night-fighter force was available, ruses were developed to divert German bombers away from their aims (*Air Warfare*, n.d.). Duplicate airfields were constructed in 1940 to withstand careful monitoring. Diversionary targets, known as 'Starfish,' were hit by innumerable bombs at the time.

Fires and lighting were recreated for industrial sites. For non-essential regions, the decision was made to use lights to re-create heavy industrial targets, as well as typical street lighting. Carbon arc lights were used to replicate tram overhead wire flashes at such sites. The fireboxes of locomotives and blast furnaces were symbolized by red LEDs. Factory skylight reflections were generated by illuminating angled wooden panels with a light source. Diversionary tactics like burning were to be carefully considered. Only until a nearby target had been bombed and the repercussions of the explosion were brought under control could begin the fake fires. If it was too early, the odds of success would have decreased; if it was too long, real fires at the target would have exceeded the diversionary fires. The boiler fire was a further advancement. The oil and water supply for these units came from two tanks situated next to each other. The flashes were comparable to those generated by the German C-250 and C-500 *Flammbomben* when water was pumped into the oil-fed burns (Academic, n.d.). The idea was to divert additional bombers away from the true target by fooling German bombardiers.

The A.R.P. went into action, and Londoners showed great endurance while not disturbing the city's work, business, and efficiency. The city's operations were hampered from time to time, although none of the city's critical services were more than momentarily affected. Social services were not drastically decreased, and public and private buildings were rebuilt as quickly as possible in cases of irreparable damage. After just a few hours of disruption, city residents were able to resume their normal routines. The Docklands district of London's East End was the primary focus of the raids. 25,000 explosives were thrown on the Port of London alone by the Germans, who saw it as a valid military target (Britannica, 2018). There were many working-class Londoners living in run-down houses in the heavily crowded and poor Docklands neighborhood. However, the attacks harmed Britain's military output, as well as the lives of many people and the displacement of many more. September 10 saw the launch of a philanthropic fund for Londoners.

On October 28, the scope of the campaign was expanded to include all of the United Kingdom and Northern Ireland, all due to donations from all over the world. By the middle of December, it had climbed to about £1,700,000 (the equivalent of approximately £100 million in 2020, adjusted for inflation).

Loge and Seeschlange

Following the bombings on September 7, fires raged in London's docklands, resulting in heavy black smoke. London's first purposeful air assaults caused extensive damage to the Port of London. In the late afternoon of September 7, 1940, the Germans launched air offensives on London and other industrial centers known as Operation London (Unternehmen Loge) and Seeschlange (Evan and Evans, 2020). 57 nights passed with Loge at the helm. The raid included 348 bombers and 617 fighters. The RAF was taken off guard by the shift in approach, which resulted in huge damage and civilian fatalities. In the Thames Estuary, 107,400 gross tons of ships were destroyed and 1,600 individuals were killed. Around 400 people were killed. In the daytime, the air battles were more fierce. Fourteen bombers and sixteen Messerschmitt Bf 109s and seven Bf 110s, as well as four reconnaissance aircraft, had been lost in the Battle of Loge. Six pilots were killed and another seven were injured, resulting in a loss of 23 aircraft for Fighter Command. Luftflotte 3 (Air Fleet 3) launched another 247 bombers that night (Talarico,

2018). The Luftwaffe returned on September 8, killing 412 people and injuring 747 more.

The Aftermath of the London Air Attack on September 9, 1940

On September 9, it seemed like the OKL was supporting two different methods. While it was attempting to force the British government to surrender immediately, it was simultaneously attempting to disrupt crucial British naval lines in order to secure a victory by siege. Heavy bombing attacks were carried out that afternoon on the London boroughs and the airport at Farnborough, despite the bad weather. Kesselring and Luftflotte 2 (Air Fleet 2) lost 24 planes, including 13 Bf 109s, during the day's action. A total of 17 aircraft and six pilots were lost by Fighter Command (USAF, n.d.). Following days of stormy weather, the next major attempt would take place on September 15, 1940. In two huge daylight raids on September 15, the Luftwaffe bombed London's ports and rail links along the Thames Estuary. If it succeeded, it would enable the Luftwaffe to overwhelm the RAF's air defenses and gain air supremacy over the British forces.

For most of the day, large-scale aerial combat took place. For three days, the train network was disrupted by the first assault, and the second attempt was a complete failure. Battle of Britain Day was created to honor the participants in the aerial conflict. That day, the Luftwaffe lost 18 percent of the bombers it sent out on missions, and it was unable to establish air supremacy. Hitler, on the other hand, was pessimistic about the Luftwaffe's chances of success. Rather than risking Germany's recently acquired military reputation on a risky cross-Channel operation, especially in the face of a skeptic Joseph Stalin in the Soviet Union, Hitler postponed Operation Sea Lion on September 17 (turns out, indefinitely).

The bombers were used as bait to attract the RAF into battle with the German fighters in the last days of the war. Even so, their efforts were ineffective; on October 7, the OKL took advantage of the deteriorating weather and the unaffordable attrition rate that came with daylight assaults.

Bomb Damage on a Birmingham Street

On October 14, Luftflotte 3 launched its biggest nighttime bombardment yet, with 380 German planes attacking London. More than 2,000 people were wounded, with an estimated death toll of 200. Anti-aircraft defenses of Britain, led by General Frederick Alfred Pile, fired 8,326 rounds and killed just two bombers. About 900 fires were ignited on October 15 when the bombers returned with a mixture of 415 short tons of high explosives and 11 short tons of incendiaries. Rolling stock was destroyed and five major train lines were shut down in London. October saw the continuation of Loge. At night, more than 6,000 short tons of bombs were dropped on the city of London alone, a total of 9,000 short tons (8,200 t). In the final 10 days of October, Birmingham and Coventry were bombarded with 500 short tons of bombs each.

Bombs that landed on Liverpool weighed 200 short tons. In addition to the attacks on Hull and Glasgow, more than 800 short tons of bombs were dropped throughout the UK. Twelve short tons (eleven metric tons) of explosives exploded at the Metropolitan-Vickers plant in Manchester. Bomber Command airfields were targeted instead of Fighter Command airfields. Firefighters battling a flame among the ruins of London's destroyed buildings following an airstrike.

There were three main objectives for the German Luftwaffe at this point: first, to continue their relentless assault on London, primarily by night attack; second, to disrupt production in West Midlands' vast industrial arms factories; and third to disrupt factories during the day by means of fighter-bombers. To strike London at night and eastern harbors in daytime, Kesselring, the commander of Luftflotte 2, was given orders to dispatch 50 aircraft every night. The Luftflotte 3 commander, Sperrle, was instructed to fly 250 sorties every night, with 100 of them flying over the West Midlands. Fliegerkorps X (10th Air Corps) would be responsible for the Seeschlange mission, which focused on mining attacks against ships. It was also a participant in the bombing raids over the United Kingdom.

On April 19/20, 1941, it dropped 3,984 mines, or one-third of the total. British admiration for the mines stemmed from their capacity to demolish whole neighborhoods, yet numerous remained unexploded in British hands, enabling the development of countermeasures that jeopardized the German anti-shipping effort. By the time the Germans modified their strategy in mid-November 1940, more than 13,000 short tons of high explosive and approximately 1,000,000 incendiaries had been dropped on London. No big raids had taken place outside of London, although there had been a lot of single-plane harassing activity and substantial diversionary strikes on Birmingham, Coventry, and Liverpool. The rails and ports of London had taken a terrible beating, and the outer railway system had been severely damaged. At one point, between 5,000 and 6,000 carriages were stranded due to the effects of delayed-action bombs on Great Britain's railroads in September.

However, the majority of traffic continued, and Londoners made it to work despite checking the list of blocked sections of line posted at their local station each morning or taking bizarre diversions through back streets in the buses. Ministry of Home Security monitors found no evidence that the morale of the troops had been weakened by the devastation of lives and property. In the months of September and October alone, more than 13,000 people were killed and almost 20,000 wounded, yet the death toll was far lower than projected. Churchill attributed the shelters' success in the late 1940s. The bombardment was seen by wartime observers as indiscriminate. This attack was imprecise and didn't strike any military objectives, but it damaged the surrounding countryside, according to Ralph Ingersoll, an American witness. According to Ingersoll, Battersea Power Station, one of London's most famous structures, was only slightly damaged (Ingersoll, 1940, p. 127).

Both Battersea and West Ham power stations were shut down on September 8, 1940, after the daytime assault on London on September 7. Even though an unneeded expansion at Battersea Power Plant was attacked and destroyed in November, the station itself remained operational during the nighttime strikes. Because the Luftwaffe couldn't properly attack particular targets during night operations, it's unclear whether the power station or any other facility was specifically targeted during the German onslaught. There was some evidence that rail and Thames bridge targets had been picked out in the early attacks on London. For example, Victoria Station was attacked four times and sustained considerable damage. The attack on London's train network caused significant delays, although no crossings were damaged. Several lines of Southern Rail were shut down on November 10 after being attacked on November 7, including St Pancras, Kensal, and Bricklayers Arms.

Throughout the month, the British government became more concerned about supply delays and disruptions. According to reports, the assaults disrupted coal shipments to the Greater London area, necessitating immediate repairs. Many Thames vessels were destroyed in the East End Docks attacks. High-explosive bombs also damaged the London Underground train system, making sections of the tunnels hazardous. Several bombs exploded near the Royal Victoria Dock, causing havoc in the Docklands and the Port of London (Forgotten Stories, 2017). Because of the bombing's high density and the ensuing combustion, firestorms with temperatures exceeding 1,800 degrees Fahrenheit had occurred. There were 'severe' but not 'crippling' losses, but the quays, basins, trains, and other equipment were still operating.

3

Improvements in British Defenses

The night air defenses of the United Kingdom were in terrible condition. Few anti-aircraft weapons were equipped with fire-control systems, and the low-powered searchlights were sometimes ineffective against aircraft flying at heights more than 12,000 feet (4,000 meters). In July 1940, just 1,200 heavy and 549 light guns were stationed across the whole United Kingdom. Of the 'heavies,' approximately 200 were the obsolete 76 mm type; the remaining were the effective 110 mm and 3.7 in 94 mm guns, with a theoretical 'ceiling' of over 29,527 feet (9,000 meters), but with a practical limit of 24,934 feet (7,600 meters) due to the predictor in users being unable to accept greater altitudes. The light guns, of which about half were of the superb Bofors 40 mm caliber, could only cope with aircraft up to 6,000 feet in altitude (Richards, n.d.).

It is now widely believed that the anti-aircraft guns were ineffective and that the falling shell fragments caused more British casualties on the ground as a result of their use, despite the fact that the use of the guns increased civilian morale in the knowledge that the German bomber crews were facing the barrage. Only a small number of fighter aircraft were capable of flying at night. Ground-based radar was limited, and aerial radar, as well as RAF night aircraft, were mostly ineffectual in the face of this situation (Manston Airfield, 2021). Even though the RAF's day fighters were transitioning to night operations, they were being replaced by the powerful Beaufighter, which was only available in limited numbers due to the conversion of the Bristol Blenheim night fighter conversion of the light bomber.

By the second month of the Blitz, the defenses were no longer functioning as effectively as they should have. General Pile, the Commander-in-Chief of Anti-Aircraft Command, was able to quickly reorganize London's defenses after the attack. It is debatable whether or not this made a difference in the efficacy of air defenses. With just 2,631 guns ready in May 1941, the British were yet one-third of the way to achieving the installation of heavy anti-aircraft artillery AAA (or ack-ack) that they had hoped for. Dowding was forced to depend on night fighters to save the day. From 1940 to 1941, the Boulton Paul Defiant was the most successful night fighter, with its four squadrons downing more enemy aircraft than any other type during that time period.

The introduction of radar and searchlights has boosted the effectiveness of anti-aircraft defenses. With time, the 20,000 rounds expended each raider shot down in September 1940 were reduced to 4,087 shells in January 1941 and to 2,963 shells in February 1941, a decrease of more than half. The reliability of Airborne Interception Radar (AI) was questionable. Because Fighter Command's resources had been depleted by the hard combat in the Battle of Britain, there was a minimal investment in night fighting. The use of airborne searchlights by bombers was done out of desperation, but the results were in vain. It was the GL (Gun Laying) radar and searchlights, in conjunction with fighter guidance from RAF fighter control rooms, that held the most promise for launching a GCI system (Ground Supervision-led Interception) under Group-level control (No. 10 Group RAF, No. 11 Group RAF, and No. 12 Group RAF) (Hooton & Internet Archive, 1999).

Sholto Douglas was appointed as Dowding's successor on November 25, after Whitehall's dissatisfaction with the RAF's shortcomings. Dowding had been set to retire at the time of the replacement. Douglas immediately went about increasing the number of squadrons and scattering the few GL sets in order to create a carpet effect across the southern regions of the United Kingdom. Despite this, only seven squadrons with 87 pilots remained in February 1941, less than half the needed strength for the mission. The GL carpet was backed up by six GCI sets, which were in charge of commanding radar-equipped night aircraft. They were growing increasingly successful by the time the Blitz reached its zenith. The number of contacts and combats increased in 1941, rising from 44 and two in 48 sorties in January 1941 to 204 and 74 in May 1941, respectively, as the war progressed (643 sorties). However, even in May, visual cat's-eye flights accounted for 67 percent of all sorties.

Contrary to popular belief, although visual sightings accounted for 43 percent of all encounters in May 1941, they were responsible for 61 percent of all combats. However, as compared to Luftwaffe daytime missions, there was a significant reduction in German losses, which fell to one percent. If a careful bomber crew was able to identify and avoid the fighter before it could strike, they had a good chance of escaping (Hooton & Internet Archive, 1999). The radar system, however, would prove to be the most important weapon in the night fights over Britain from this point on. Dowding had pioneered the idea of airborne radar and advocated for its widespread use. It was inevitable that it would become a success. The Fighter Interception Unit's Flying Officer Cyril Ashfield, Pilot Officer Geoffrey Morris (air observer), and Flight Sergeant Reginald Leyland (Air Intercept radar operator) made history on the night of 22/23 of July, 1940, when their AI night fighter brought down a Do 17 off the coast of Sussex, becoming the first pilot and crew to do so using onboard radar to guide them to a visual intercept (White, 2007).

Dowding's prediction came true when, on November 19, 1940, the legendary RAF night fighter ace John Cunningham used airborne radar to bring down a Junkers Ju-88 bomber. By the middle of November, nine squadrons were available, but only one of them was equipped with Beaufighter fighter planes (No. 219 Squadron RAF at RAF Kenley). By the 16th of February 1941, the number had increased to 12, with five

Beaufighters fully or partly equipped, divided across 5 Groups, being deployed.

Night Assaults in the Second Phase

By February 1941, the Luftwaffe had changed its tactics and was attacking other industrial cities. The West Midlands, in particular, has been singled out. He 111s from Kampfgeschwader 26 (the 26th Bomber Wing, or KG 26) struck London on November 13 and 14, while 63 He 111s from Kampfgeschwader 55 targeted Birmingham on the same night. The next night, a significant amount of force descended on Coventry. Pathfinders from 12 Kampfgruppe 100 (Bomb Group 100 or KGr 100) led 437 bombers from KG 1, KG 3, KG 26, KG 27, KG 55, and Lehrgeschwader 1 (1st Training Wing, or LG 1) in the dropping of 394 short tons of high explosive, 56 short tons of incendiaries, and 127 parachute mines over the German city of Dresden. According to some reports, 449 bombers and a total of 530 short tons of bombs were used in the attack.

The attack on Coventry was especially damaging, and the word "to coventrate" became widely used as a result of the incident. More than 10,000 incendiaries were dropped in all. In Coventry, around 21 industries were severely destroyed, and the loss of public utilities caused work to be suspended at nine others, causing industrial production to be disrupted for many months. Despite the fact that the RAF flew 125-night missions, only one bomber was lost, which was shot down by the anti-aircraft fire. As a result of OKL's miscalculation about the British ability to recover, no more attacks were carried out (as Bomber Command would do over Germany from 1943 to 1945) (Hooton & Internet Archive, 1999). The success of the strike took the Germans completely by surprise. The operation had a strategic consequence in that it caused a temporary 20 percent decrease in aircraft production.

Five nights later, 369 bombs from KG 54, KG 26, and KG 55 struck Birmingham, killing 369 people. By the end of November, 1,100 bombers were ready to launch night strikes on targets throughout Europe. Every night, an average of 200 people were able to strike. A total of 13,900 short tons of bombs were dropped by the Luftwaffe during this two-month period of intense bombardment. In November 1940, more than 6,000 sorties and 23 large strikes (including the dropping of more than 100 tons of bombs) were carried out. In addition, two massive (50 short tons of bombs) strikes were carried out by helicopter. In December, only 11 major and five heavy assaults were launched, bringing the total to five.

German aircraft attacked the City of London itself with incendiary and high explosive bombs on the evening of December 29, generating a firestorm that has come to be known as the Second Great Fire of London. This was the most damaging assault, and it was the most widespread. The first unit to use these incendiaries was Kampfgruppe 100, which sent a total of ten He 111 'pathfinder' bombers. It dropped the first of 10,000 firebombs at 18:17, with a total of 300 bombs dropped each minute throughout the course of the mission. Approximately 130 German bombers demolished the historic center of London. There were 28,556 civilian deaths and 25,578 civilian injuries in London during the Blitz, according to official figures. The Luftwaffe had dropped a total of 18,291 short tons of bombs during World War II. A significant portion of the Luftwaffe's effort was directed toward inland cities. Attempts were made to target port cities in order to impede commerce and maritime communications. Swansea was bombed four times in January, each time with a high level of damage. On January 17, over 100 aircraft dropped a high concentration of incendiaries, totaling around 32,000 incendiaries.

The business and residential districts were the most severely affected by the storm. Four days later, 230 tons of explosives, including 60,000 incendiaries, were dropped. In Portsmouth, Southsea, and Gosport, waves of 150 aircraft dropped 40,000 incendiaries on huge areas of the city, causing widespread devastation. Warehouses, train lines, and residences were all destroyed or severely damaged, while the ports escaped with little damage (Ray & Internet Archive, 2000). In January and February 1941, the Luftwaffe's serviceability rates plummeted to the point where just 551 out of 1,214 bombers were combat-capable. Seven large and eight heavy assaults were carried out, although the weather conditions made it impossible to maintain the level of intensity. Nonetheless, the strikes on Southampton were so powerful that morale was momentarily eroded, with civilian authorities escorting people out of the city in large numbers.

Despite the fact that official German air policy aimed to boost civilian morale, it did not advocate for the direct assault on civilian targets. With the goal of damaging the enemy's industry and public utilities, as well as its food supplies, it set out to devastate morale (by attacking shipping). Nonetheless, the government's public objection to assaults on people became debatable when large-scale operations were carried out in November and December 1940, causing the issue to become increasingly irrelevant. However, despite the fact that it was not supported by official policy, the employment of mines and incendiaries for tactical purposes came dangerously close to indiscriminate bombing. Locating targets in skies shrouded by industrial haze necessitated the illumination of the target area and the use of weapons "without regard for the civilian population" (Hooton & Internet Archive, 1999).

Incendiaries and high explosives were utilized to denote the location of the target area by special units such as KGr 100, which became known as the *Beleuchtergruppe* (Firelighter Group). *Fireleitung* (Blaze Control) was developed as a result of the development of *Brandbombenfelder* (Incendiary Fields), which were used to identify and designate targets. These were distinguished by the use of parachute flares. Streets and residential areas were leveled by bombers wielding 'Satan' bombs of various weights, including the SC 1000 (2,204 pounds) , the SC 1400 (6,803 pounds), and the SC 1800 (3,969 pounds). By the end of December, the SC 2500 (5,511 pounds) "Max" bomb had been used.

The result of these choices, which seemed to have been made at the Luftflotte or Fliegerkorps level, was that assaults on specific targets were progressively supplanted by what was, for all intents and purposes, an unrestricted area attack, also known as a *Terrorangriff* (Terror Attack). The inaccuracy of navigation was a contributing factor to this outcome. Because of the efficiency of British countermeasures against Knicke-bein, the Luftwaffe began to rely on firelight for target marking and navigation rather than a radar system. The move from precision bombing to area assault may be seen in the tactical approaches used and the weapons that have been deployed. KGr 100 raised its usage of incendiaries from 13 to 28 percent throughout the course of the year.

By the end of the year, the figure had risen to 92 percent. It was evident from the use of incendiaries, which were inherently incorrect, that far less care was taken to prevent destroying civilian property in the vicinity of industrial installations. Other troops discontinued the use of parachute flares and instead relied on explosive target markers to designate their positions. German aircrews who were captured said that the residences of industrial employees had been targeted on purpose as well. The Royal Air Force conducted two massive night strikes on ships in Tripoli's international harbor. Bombs straddle the southeast mole, which also had five cruise ships docked. Firefighters were called to the scene of a fire at the customs jetty, which also included many ships, including two huge motorboats. Several more attacks against the city of Bardia were being carried out in the Western Desert. In the meanwhile, preparations for the ground attack were still underway.

Bremen was under attack from the air, which was a welcome sight closer to home. A total of 20,000 incendiaries, as well as a considerable quantity of high-explosive bombs, were dropped throughout the operation. The Germans, on the other hand, conducted raids on London and Merseyside. There were also a few bombs that were strangely dropped in Ireland, and further investigations revealed that they were German-made.

4

Final Attacks The Luftwaffe changed it

T he Luftwaffe changed its tactics again in 1941. As the Kriegsmarine's commander in chief, Erich Raeder had long maintained that the Luftwaffe should aid the German submarine force (U-Bootwaffe) in the Battle of the Atlantic by targeting ships in the Atlantic Ocean and assaulting British ports. Eventually, he was able to persuade Hitler that it was necessary to target British port infrastructure (Overy & Internet Archive, 2005). At Raeder's instigation, Hitler correctly observed that the destruction of merchant shipping by submarines and air attacks by small numbers of Focke-Wulf Fw 200 naval aircraft had caused the greatest damage to the British war economy, and he ordered the German air arm to concentrate its efforts against British convoys.

As a result, coastal areas in the United Kingdom and ships in the North Sea west of Ireland were the primary targets. When Hitler expressed an interest in this plan in January 1941, Göring and Jeschonnek were compelled to evaluate the air campaign against Britain. It was as a result of this that the Allies agreed to Hitler's Directive 23, Directions for operations against the British War Economy, which was issued on February 6, 1941 and assigned the highest priority to aircraft interdiction of British imports by sea (Hooton & Internet Archive, 1999).

Despite the fact that this approach had been recognized before the war, Operation Eagle Attack and the subsequent Battle of Britain had gotten in the way of attacking Britain's naval lines and diverting German air power to the assault against the RAF and its supporting infrastructure. Interdiction of maritime communications had always been seen as less important than attacking land-based aircraft manufacturing facilities by the OKL. Directive 23 was the single concession made by Göring to the Kriegsmarine in regard to the Luftwaffe's strategic bombing plan against the United Kingdom during World War II. Following that, he would refuse to make any air units available to target British dockyards, ports, port infrastructure, or commerce in the dock or at sea, fearing that the Kriegsmarine would take control of additional Luftwaffe units as a result (Overy & Internet Archive, 2005).

Raeder's replacement, Karl Dönitz, would acquire control of one unit (KG 40) when Hitler intervened, but Göring would retake control of the unit within a few months. Goering's unwillingness to cooperate was harmful to the one airplane, which had the potential to have a decisive strategic impact on Britain.

Instead, he squandered the resources of Fliegerführer Atlantik (Flying Command Atlantic) by bombing the British Isles rather than launching assaults on supply convoys (Murray, 1983). He believed that his reputation had been harmed by the Battle of Britain's loss and that the only way to restore it was by subduing Britain with the air force alone. Raeder was someone with whom he had a difficult relationship. Although the OKL decided to accept Directive 23 as a result of two factors, neither of which had anything to do with the desire to destroy the United Kingdom's maritime communications in collaboration with the Kriegsmarine, they were still important factors to take into account. After realizing that predicting the effect of bombing on war production was impossible, and after concluding that British morale was unlikely to collapse, the OKL decided to pursue a navy-based strategy (Hooton & Internet Archive, 1999).

The OKL's disinterest in Directive 23 was arguably most evident in the operational directives that were issued to mitigate its impact. They emphasized that their primary strategic goal was in assaulting ports, but they focused on keeping pressure on or redirecting strength to industries that produced airplanes, anti-aircraft artillery, and explosives in order to do this. If the main targets are unable to be assaulted due to weather circumstances, other options will be investigated (Hooton & Internet Archive, 1999).

The command went on to state that not only should the enemy suffer the greatest amount of casualties possible, but that the air war should be intensified in order to give the appearance that an amphibious attack on Britain was planned for 1941. However, the weather conditions over the United Kingdom were unfavorable for flying, and an increase in aviation operations was not allowed to proceed. Due to flooding, the Luftwaffe's Kampfgeschwadern (bomber wings) were forced to transfer to Germany for rest and re-equipment. The Luftwaffe's 18 Kampfgruppen (bomber groups) were relocated to Germany for relaxation and re-equipment (Hooton & Internet Archive, 1999).

Ports in the United Kingdom

From the German point of view, the month of March 1941 saw a significant improvement. There were 4,000 sorties flown by the Luftwaffe in that month, including 12 major and three heavy raids. The electronic battle became more intense, but the Luftwaffe was only able to fly significant interior operations at night because of the moonlight. Ports were simpler to locate and hence made for excellent targets. Radio silence was kept until the bombs were dropped in order to confound the British. The X- and Y-Gerät beams were put over fictitious targets and swapped just at the last minute to reveal the real ones. In order to keep X-Gerät operational, rapid frequency adjustments were used. Its larger spectrum of frequencies and better tactical flexibility allowed it to stay operational at a time when British selective jamming was reducing the efficacy of Y-Gerät (Hooton & Internet Archive, 1999).

Because the Luftwaffe had failed to achieve the necessary air supremacy, the impending danger of invasion had all but vanished by this point. In addition to destroying industrial targets, the aerial bombardment continued with the goal of weakening the morale of the civilian population, which was achieved in part by using a more indiscriminate approach (Murray, 1983). During the month of March, the assaults were concentrated on western ports. These assaults resulted in a few lapses in morale, with civic officials abandoning the city before the on-slaught reached its pinnacle of intensity. As seven Kampfgruppen relo-cated to Austria in preparation for the Balkans Campaign, which would take place in Yugoslavia and Greece, Luftwaffe's efforts slowed in the re-maining ten raids. Because of a scarcity of bombers, OKL was forced to improvise. A total of 50 Junkers Ju 87 Stuka dive-bombers and Jabos (fighter-bombers) were utilized, which were officially classified as *Leichte Kampfflugzeuge* ("light bombers") but were also referred to as *Leichte Kesselringe* (Light Rings) in certain circles ("Light Kesselring's").

The defenses were unable to prevent massive destruction, although they were successful in preventing German bombers from focusing on their objectives on several occasions. It was not uncommon for barely one-third of German bombs to strike their intended objectives (Hooton & Internet Archive, 1999).

When Bombings Hit Liverpool's Downtown Center

As a result of the diversion of heavier bombers to the Balkans, the crews and units left behind were required to fly two or three sorties every night, depending on the situation. It was difficult to sleep in bombers since they were loud, chilly, and vibrated excessively. In addition to the stress of the operation, which taxed and depleted the personnel, fatigue caught up with and killed several of them. On April 28 and 29, Peter Stahl of KG 30 was flying his 50th mission when he was involved in an incident. While flying in his Ju-88, he fell asleep at the controls, only to awaken to find his whole crew sleeping. It was his responsibility to wake them up, make sure they had oxygen and Dextro-Energen pills, and then execute the task. The Luftwaffe was still capable of causing sig-nificant damage, and following Germany's conquest of Western Europe, the German air and submarine offensive against British sea communications became significantly more dangerous than the German offensive against British sea communications during the First World War.

As a result of this, Liverpool and its port became a popular destination for convoys carrying supplies and materiel from North America across the Western Approaches. It is possible to travel across the nation because of the extensive train network. Airstrikes caused the loss of 39,126 long tons of shipping, as well as the damage of another 111,601 long tons of cargo. The Minister for Home Security, Herbert Morrison, was similarly concerned that morale was eroding, citing the defeatism voiced by citizens as evidence of this concern. According to some reports, half of the port's 144 berths have been rendered unusable, and the port's cargo unloading capacity has been cut by 75%. Roads and railroads were closed, and ships were unable to depart the port area. On May 8, 1941, a total of 57 ships were destroyed, sunk, or damaged, resulting in a loss of 80,000 long tons of cargo (81,000 t).

On a single night, around 66,000 homes were demolished and 77,000 people were forced to flee (referred to as "bombed out"), with 1,900 people dead and 1,450 critically injured. Up to May 1941, operations against London had the potential to have a negative influence on morale. The population of the port of Hull was known as "trekkers," a term used to describe individuals who fled cities in large numbers before, during, and after invasions. The Luftwaffe's strikes failed to bring down railroads or port infrastructure for an extended period of time, especially at the Port of London, which had been the focus of several attacks (Overy & Internet Archive, 2005). The Port of London, in particular, was a significant target since it accounted for one-third of all international commerce. The upper Clyde port of Clydebank, which is near Glasgow, was bombarded on March 13 (Clydebank Blitz). All but seven of the city's 12,000 dwellings were destroyed. A large number of other ports were attacked. Prior to the conclusion of the month, Plymouth was assaulted five times, while Belfast, Hull, and Cardiff were also targeted.

Cardiff was bombarded three nights in a row, while the center of Portsmouth was destroyed by five strikes. In September 1940, the pace of civilian housing loss averaged 40,000 persons per week, with an average of 40,000 people unsheltered every week. Two attacks on Plymouth and London in March 1941 resulted in the deportation of 148,000 persons (Angus Calder, 1997). Despite this, British ports continued to assist the war industry, and supplies from North America continued to travel through them, while the Royal Navy continued to operate out of the ports of Plymouth, Southampton, and Portsmouth, despite the devastation they had sustained (Angus Calder, 1997). Plymouth in particular, due to its strategically important location on the south coast and its closeness to German air bases, was exposed to the most intense bombardment throughout the war.

On March 10 and 11, 240 bombers dropped 193 tons of heavy explosives and 46,000 incendiaries, causing widespread destruction. A large number of dwellings and commercial buildings were severely damaged, the power supply was disrupted, as well as five oil tanks and two magazines exploded. Approximately nine days later, two waves of 125 and 170 aircraft dropped large bombs, containing 160 tons of high explosives and 32,000 incendiaries, in separate waves. A large portion of the city center was destroyed. However, numerous bombs were dropped on the city proper, causing significant damage to port infrastructure. KG 26 commanded a squadron of 250 bombers that dropped 346 tons of bombs and 46,000 incendiaries on the city of Dresden on April 17.

The damage was extensive, and the Germans also deployed aerial mines. A total of almost 2,000 AAA rounds were fired, resulting in the destruction of two Ju-88 fighters (Ray, 2000). The use of mines against British ports accounted for barely eight percent of the German effort against British ports by the time the air campaign over Britain was ended. During the massive attack on the 10 and 11th of May, firefighters were forced to operate amid burning structures.

Efforts were concentrated in the north towards Newcastle-upon-Tyne and Sunderland, two significant ports on the English east coast that were targeted for destruction. On April 9, 1941, Luftflotte 2 launched a five-hour assault with 120 aircraft, dropping 150 tons of high explosives and 50,000 incendiaries in the process. Sewer, rail, docklands, and power infrastructure were all harmed as a result. On April 25, Luftflotte 2 dropped 80 tons of high explosives and 9,000 incendiaries on Sunderland, resulting in the deaths of 9,000 people. There has been a great deal of destruction. On the 6th and 7th of May, a second assault on the Clyde, this time at Greenock, was launched. However, as was the case with the assaults in the south, the Germans were unable to impede marine traffic or cripple the industrial sectors in the affected areas.

The final big assault on London occurred on the night of May 10/11, 1941, during which the Luftwaffe flew 571 flights and dropped 800 tons of bombs on the capital. More than 2,000 fires were started as a result, and 1,436 people were killed and 1,792 severely wounded, which had a negative impact on morale. On the 11th and 12th of May, 1941, another attack was carried out (Hooton & Internet Archive, 1999). Westminster Abbey and the Law Courts were both damaged, while the Chamber of the House of Commons was completely destroyed. One-third of London's streets were inaccessible due to the flooding. For many weeks, all but one of the train station lines were shut down. It was a noteworthy operation since it included the dispatch of 63 German aircraft with the bombers, demonstrating the increasing efficiency of RAF night fighter defenses.

Night Fighters From the Royal Air Force

German air superiority throughout the night was now also in jeopardy. The success of British night-fighter operations over the English Channel was proving to be a boon. Initially, this did not seem to be true. In the Bristol Blenheim F.1 were four .303 in (7.7 mm) machine guns, which were not powerful enough to take down a Do 17, Ju-88, or Heinkel He 111 with ease. A modest speed advantage allowed the Blenheim to overtake a German bomber in a stern chase, but it was not enough. A kill was quite improbable even under the circumstances of a moonlight sky due to the fact that an interception was dependent on visual sightings alone. Despite its poor performance during daylight conflicts, the Boulton Paul Defiant was a far superior night fighter than its daytime counterpart. In addition to being quicker and more capable of catching bombers, its turret layout of four machine guns allowed it to attack the German bomber from below, similar to the arrangement used by German night fighters during the period 1943–1945.

A bigger target was available while attacking from below as opposed to assaulting tail-on. Additionally, there was a higher possibility of not being seen by the crew (and therefore less probability of escape), as well as a greater potential of detonating its bomb load. In the following months, a consistent number of German bombers would be shot down by night fighters (Mackay, 2003). As a result of the Bristol Beaufighter, which was then under development, improved aircraft designs were on the way. It would prove to be a powerful opponent, but its progress was glacial (Mackay, 2003).

With a top speed of 320 miles per hour (510 kilometers per hour), an operational ceiling of 26,000 feet (7,900 meters), and a climb rate of 2,500 feet (760 meters) per minute, the Beaufighter's battery of four 20 mm (0.79 in) Hispano cannon and six .303 in Browning machine guns was significantly more lethal. A bomber piloted by an AI-equipped Beaufighter was shot down by John Cunningham of No. 604 Squadron RAF on November 19, marking the first air victory for the airborne radar system (Mackay, 2003). During the months of November and December 1940, the Luftwaffe conducted 9,000 sorties against British objectives, with just six of those aircraft being shot down by RAF night fighters. In January 1941, Fighter Command flew 486 sorties, compared to the Germans' 1,965 sorties during the same month. The RAF and the AA defenses were able to claim just three and twelve aircraft, respectively (Ray, 2000). The Luftwaffe flew 1,644 sorties in February 1941, despite the poor weather conditions. Fighter Command launched 568 sorties in February 1941 to match this total. Only four bombers were claimed by night fighters, resulting in four casualties.

It was still possible for the Luftwaffe to reach their objectives in April and May 1941 with losses of just one to two percent each operation in these months (Mackay, 2003). On the night of April 19/20, 1941, in celebration of Hitler's 52nd birthday, 712 bombers attacked Plymouth, dropping a total of 1,000 tons of bombs. Losses were kept to a bare minimum. A total of 22 German bombers were lost in the next month, with 13 of them being verified to have been shot down by night fighters. On the night of the 3rd and 4th of May, nine people were killed by gunfire.

On the night of May 10/11, London was severely damaged, but ten German aircraft were shot down. In May 1941, night fighters from the Royal Air Force knocked down 38 German bombers. In late May, Kesselring's Luftflotte 2 was disbanded, leaving Hugo Sperrle's Luftflotte 3 as a token force to keep the idea of strategic bombing alive (Hooton & Internet Archive, 1999). Hitler's attention was now focused on assaulting the Soviet Union with Operation Barbarossa, and the Blitz was officially over.

5

Bombing of Germans on Other Cities

The Second World War is often referred to as "Hitler's war." The Germans were so victorious in the first 2 years of the Third Reich that Hitler almost achieved his goal of establishing dominance throughout Europe. His victories, on the other hand, were not a factor in the larger strategic vision that ensured success in the extended term. Despite this, the early victories were spectacular in nature. Hitler's attention was drawn toward the west after he had defeated Poland in less than a month. He felt that the defeat of France and Britain was required before he could shift his attention towards the east to the regions that were to provide the "living space" for his future empire. The attacks on the Western Front started in the spring of 1940 and continued until the end of the year. Hitler invaded Denmark and Norway in the course of a few days in April, and on May 10, he did an assault on France, as well as Luxembourg, Belgium, and the Netherlands, as part of his campaign against the Allies (Geary *et al.*, 2022).

As in the last campaign, his soldiers gained quick successes; Luxembourg, Belgium, and the Netherlands were captured in a few days, and France surrendered on June 21. Only the British, who were now on their own, stood in Hitler's way of achieving absolute victory in the West. Nothing could possibly compare to the courage of the hundreds of soldiers who flew and died as part of Bomber Command. The fatality rate was an excessive 44 percent. Many historians question how it could be appropriate for the Allies to have intentionally targeted German cities, resulting in the deaths of hundreds of thousands of civilians. Although the operation was successful on a tactical level, it failed to bring about the collapse in civilian morale that it had hoped to achieve.

Many others, on the other hand, believe that the assaults made a major contribution to the Allied success. The German army and air force were diverted away from the eastern and western fronts, and the German air force was largely decimated by Allied bombing operations, paving the way for the invasion of continental Europe (Bamford, 2020).

Hitler was certain that he could eliminate Britain from the war by using the air force alone. German bombers launched their assault on the United Kingdom in August 1940, but the British proved to be unbeatable. The German air force was unable to bring Britain to its knees, partly due to the superior power of the British air force, partly due to the German air force's inadequacy for the mission, and partly due to the British ability to decrypt German code (Overy *et al.*, 2016). But Hitler was so sure of his ability to achieve a fast victory that, even before the attack started, he directed his military strategists to begin laying the groundwork for an invasion of the Soviet Union. He decided to attack on May 15, 1941, for the invasion.

A major strategic aim for Nazi Germany in 1941 was the destruction of the Soviet Union. However, during the early months of 1941, Hitler allowed himself to get distracted by two wars, which caused his invasion to be postponed. His partner Mussolini was experiencing military problems on both occasions, and he felt obligated to assist him. Mussolini had invaded Greece in October 1940, despite knowing that he was already in trouble in North Africa, where he had been unable to cut off Britain's Mediterranean lifeline in Egypt and in Greece (Zabecki, 2006). In February 1941, Hitler decided to deploy an armored division under the leadership of General Erwin Rommel to North Africa in order to assist Mussolini in his campaign against the Axis powers.

When Mussolini's invasion of Greece became stalemated as well, Hitler decided to dispatch troops once again. In order to get to Greece,

German forces had to pass through the Balkan nations, which were all legally neutral at the time. Hitler was successful in pressuring these nations into agreeing to the passage of German forces. However, on March 27, a revolt in Yugoslavia ousted the government, and the country's new authorities reneged on their commitment to the pact. In retribution, Hitler began an operation against the Yugoslavs that he dubbed Operation Punishment. The Yugoslav resistance crumbled rapidly, and as a result, the intended invasion of the Soviet Union was delayed for another month.

Places Affected by the German Bombing

The places that were affected the most by the German Bombing were:

St. Dunstan's Church in the City of London

Long before the outbreak of the Second World War, the British government expressed grave anxiety about the likelihood of air attacks in the event of a future battle. The previous prime minister Stanley Baldwin had issued a warning in 1932, stating that "the bomber would always get through." Aerial devastation had been shown during the Spanish Civil War, and by the time Britain entered the war with Germany, many people feared a worldwide disaster. In a 60-day attack, it was predicted that 1.8 million people would die or be harmed, according to estimates from two years ago. To find out whether or not their darkest fears will come true, the citizens of the United Kingdom had to wait a whole year! After two waves of German bombers dropped their payloads over London on September 7, 1940, the Blitz officially began, claiming the lives of or hurting more than 2,000 people and causing the greatest fires the city had seen since 1666.

The docklands in London's East End were the primary target at the time, as they would be on numerous subsequent occasions. On the first day of the Blitz, the neighborhood of Stepney was subjected to a terrible mauling. Bernard Kops, who was a resident in the neighborhood in 1940, subsequently recalled the event, saying, "That day stands out like a flaming wound in my memory. Imagine a ground floor flat crowded with hysterical women, crying babies, and great crashes in the sky and the whole earth-shaking" (*Your Guide to the Blitz, plus 9 Places Affected by the Bombings,* 2020).

Although many of the buildings in Stepney were destroyed during the Blitz, the church of St Dunstan and All Saints was able to remain standing with just its windows shattered. Even though the church's main construction is mostly late medieval, it is one of London's oldest, having been in existence since the ninth century (*Your Guide to the Blitz, plus 9 Places Affected by the Bombings,* 2020). Currently, one of the church's stained-glass windows commemorates the Second World War, depicting an image of Jesus rising over the wreckage of Stepney after the Blitz.

Chislehurst Caves

People took refuge from the bombs in these locations. Over the period of many thousand years, this ancient cave complex has been progressively excavated from the rock under the surface. Chislehurst was a chalk mining town until the early nineteenth century, after which it developed into a renowned tourist destination, which it continues to be to this day (*Your Guide to the Blitz, plus 9 Places Affected by the Bombings,* 2020). During the Second World War, however, the caverns became very popular for a completely opposite reason: they were used as a hospital.

Londoners who were forced to endure the Blitz were in dire need of protection. Anderson shelters had been distributed by the government to hundreds of thousands of homes, but they gave very little protection and were only accessible to those who had gardens. The indoor Morrison shelter was not made available to the public until March of 1941 (*Your Guide to the Blitz, plus 9 Places Affected by the Bombings,* 2020). As a result, a large number of residents sought refuge in other locations as aircraft descended from the sky night after night.

Chislehurst Caves was transformed into a massive makeshift air-raid shelter in this spirit. There were so many Londoners making use of the caves and passages that special trains were needed to take them all there. As an eyewitness noticed in November 1940, some people even settled down and made themselves comfortable. "We were told to go to the inner caves: but they had been filled by regular visitors—who had commandeered positions weeks before. Some had taken possession of cut-out rooms, and curtains were fixed in front and behind... there were tables, cooking stoves, beds, and chairs behind the curtains. Bombed out families live there permanently and the father goes to work and returns there and the mother goes out to shop and that is their home" (*Your Guide to the Blitz, plus 9 Places Affected by the Bombings,* 2020). Bombs from World War II still lie unexploded in Germany, amounting to tens of thousands of metric tons.

In spite of being deployed in Europe more than 70 years ago, the ordnance continues to inflict misery and destruction on its victims. American and British aircraft dropped more than two million tons of bombs on Germany between 1940 and 1945 (*Every bomb dropped by the British & Americans during WW2,* 2017). By the time the Nazi leadership surrendered in May 1945, dozens of German cities had been reduced to cinder and ash moonscapes, including railheads, munitions industries, and oil refineries.

After the Allies seized power, reconstruction began almost immediately. Many bombs dropped by the Allies did not go off, and hundreds of tons of unexploded ordnance lay scattered over East and West Germany as a result. There were bomb disposal teams made up of police officers and firefighters called the *Kampfmittelbeseitigungsdienst* (or KMBD) who worked on both sides to remove unexploded ordnance as well as thousands of other types of weapons that had been left behind by the end of World War II.

Even after 70 years after the conclusion of World War II, more than 2,000 tons of unexploded ordnance are being discovered on German soil. Before beginning any construction project in Germany, the ground must be cleared of explosive bombs. This includes everything from a new home to a national railroad. However, in May of last year, police in Cologne were forced to evacuate over 20,000 people when a one-ton bomb was discovered during construction work. The 'Blockbuster' bomb in Dortmund, Germany, was defused in November 2013, result-ing in the evacuation of an additional 20,000 people. Drought in 2011 unearthed a similar device at Koblenz on the Rhine's bed, resulting in the country's largest evacuation since World War II: 45,000 Germans fled their homes. Despite the fact that Germany has been at peace for three decades, its bomb disposal units remain among the busiest in the world. Tried and true methods of disarming an explosive weighing one thousand pounds were used in 2010 at a prominent *Göttingen* flea mar-ket.

An official from Brandenburg's state bomb disposal unit KMBD told one winter morning that 30 years after starting his bomb disposal career, it never occurred to him that he'd still be doing it in 2016. De-spite this, his men uncover and destroy one aerial bomb every few weeks, resulting in an annual finding of more than 500 tons of unexploded mu-nitions. According to him, there are still a lot of bombs buried under the surface. Because of the events of 70 years ago, unexploded bombs continue to be a danger in one of his territory's cities every single day. If you're looking for something more exciting than the normal Mc-Donald's with a tubular thicket of bicycles parked outside the fast-food establishment on the main street, this is the place for you. The most dan-gerous German city, according to Reinhardt, is Oranienburg.

More than 600 planes from the Eighth Air Force dropped 1,500 tons of high explosives over Oranienburg, a major target area that con-tained rail yards, a Heinkel aircraft factory, and two chemical conglom-erates Auergesellschaft factories positioned on each side of the rail yards (Higginbotham, 2016). Early in 1945, US intelligence discovered that the Auergesellschaft Oranienburg factory had begun manufacturing enriched uranium, a key component of the atomic bomb's primary fuel source. It was General Leslie Groves who personally authorized the March 15 attack, which was aimed at preventing Nazi nuclear research from coming into the hands of rapidly approaching Russian troops. In comparison to the other 12 air assaults, this one was the most damaging.

6

Life During the Blitz

Bad nights, awful nights, and better nights were all that mattered to Londoners at the time. During the war's first week, no one had gotten much sleep. Around the same time every night, the sirens would sound, and in the poorest areas, people would gather in front of air-raid shelters to prepare for an emergency (Panter-Downes, 1940). The Blitzkrieg continued to target military targets such as the exhausted shopgirl, the red-eyed clerk, and the thousands of disoriented and weary people slowly trundling their meager goods in perambulators out from the devastation of their houses.

After a couple of these sleepless nights, a strange form of sleep came from tiredness alone. The most remarkable aspect of the situation was the cheerfulness and tenacity of the people who were performing their duties under stressful situations. Their faces were well-groomed and they served tea or sold them a hat as cheerfully as usual, even if the girls had taken twice as long to get there. Small business owners whose windows had been blasted out swapped banter with their customers while putting up "Business as normal" stickers on their walls. Despite the fact that the London Blitz occurred over eighty years ago and across an ocean, the majority of Americans remember it as a moment when the people of London joined together across socioeconomic lines, held their heads up, and refused to fear (Gershon, 2018).

Geoffrey Field, a historian, demonstrates that the truth is more convoluted. Fields writes that Londoners "kept calm and carried on" to some extent (a slogan, incidentally, that the public never saw during the war) (Gershon, 2018). There were far more "bomb neuroses" cases than expected, yet just two persons a week showed up in emergency departments with serious psychiatric symptoms. This surprised psychiatrists. In contrast, there were reports of anxiety attacks, tic disorders, stomach ulcers, miscarriages, and brain hemorrhages. There was a disparity in the amount of pain felt. Britain's authorities had considered how London's destitute East End, which was home to large numbers of Jews and immigrants, may become unstable in the face of a bombing campaign (Gershon, 2018). In fact, those were the areas where there were fewer shelters than necessary. More than a quarter of a million people were temporarily displaced as a result of the bombing in the first six weeks after it occurred.

Children in the United Kingdom experienced a great deal of turmoil during World War II. More than a million people were forced to flee their homes and make new ones far away from their loved ones. Those who remained were subjected to bombings, and many were either wounded or forced to flee their homes. In the face of the prospect of chemical attack, air raid precautions (ARP), rationing, and other life-altering developments, everyone had to cope (IWM, 2018a). The Luftwaffe dropped more than 13,000 tons of bombs and 12,000 incendiary canisters on London every night from September 7 until mid-November, yet the German casualties were rising and the British morale remained strong.. More than 400 German aircraft were brought down in the last three weeks of September as the weather worsened and the days became shorter. In October, a frustrated Hitler canceled his invasion preparations and shifted his focus.

Londoners had a difficult time during World War II, which lasted from 1939 to 1945. There was a severe shortage of both food and clothes. Fear, injury, death, and damage resulted from the bombing. Due to evacuations and dads going to war, families were frequently separated. Uncertainty and misery were a part of life in London (Panter-Downes, 1940). It is true that in certain ways, the London Underground shelters promoted interclass unity. As a result of the midnight bombs, the authorities soon relented after first trying to prevent people from utilizing London Tube stations as a refuge. Some families were regulars at the stations, while others only came up when the bombing was very intense. On any given night, between 100,000 and 150,000 individuals may be found in the stations.

Churchmen or air-raid guards, or even the families who had taken refuge in the stations, eventually formed their own mini-governments. Disinfectants were collected, smoking and children's play and sleeping areas were partitioned, and committees were formed in order to mediate disagreements or exert pressure on the authorities. Even station committees had conferences in order to exchange ideas. Some authorities were concerned about self-organization. For their own benefit and to organize dances and entertainment, homeless individuals in shelters are increasingly forming self-governing committees. These committees frequently take on a communist slant.

Even in the Stepney neighborhood of London, where the Communist Party had previously been associated with local tenant organizations, Field reports that Communists participated in a number of shelter committees. In January 1941, members of Shelter joined the People's Convention, which was held by the Soviet Union. However, the London shelters did in some ways encourage cross-class cooperation. The nation's upper and middle classes were exposed to positive depictions of the working class from the shelters. Pro-British and socialist themes coexisted in the work of numerous wartime London journalists, including George Orwell,

"Slatternly malodorous tatterdemalions trailing children to match" was how historian R.C.K. Ensor described destitute London moms a year before this. In the past, the slums were depicted by photographers, painters, and authors with calm dignity. The moment they stood for the country, like London itself, they did so, according to Field.

Here's what it was like for kids to grow up during World War II.

War's Dominating Threat

The rise of Nazism in Europe in the 1930s posed a growing threat to peace. Preparedness for another war started in Britain. Detailed preparations for Air Raid Precautions (ARP) were set up since it was believed that air raids and chemical attacks would be launched against populations. Precautions were taken during the Munich Crisis of 1938 when war looked near. Residents received air raid shelters, a nighttime blackout, and 38 million gas masks were made available. Arrangements had been made as well for the mass exodus of children from populated areas. Around this time, 4,000 'Ninos,' or Spanish youngsters displaced by the struggle against fascism, found refuge in the United Kingdom. From December 1938 forward, almost 10,000 Jewish children from Germany, Austria, and Czechoslovakia were transported to the United Kingdom by their parents in order to avoid Nazi persecution (Francois, 2018).

Evacuation

The British government started removing children from towns and cities on September 1, 1939, two days before the war was declared. It was the biggest migration of people ever witnessed in Britain. Most of the students went to live with foster parents after they left school by train (IWM, 2018a). Some people found the evacuation exciting because it was their first time venturing into the countryside, but others were miserable because they missed their homes. Inner-city children's terrible hygiene and food have startled foster parents. Others were forced to relocate to remote, primitive rural settlements without access to modern conveniences. Many refugees returned to their homes during this early period, called the "Phoney War," because of the lack of airstrikes. Thousands of children were evacuated to North America, Australia, New Zealand, and South Africa as a result of the invasion of France and the beginning of airstrikes on Britain.

The Summer of the Spitfires

In 1940, there was a serious danger that Britain might be attacked after France's defeat in the summer of 1940. The Nazis conquered the Channel Islands in early July, and the islanders were forced to live under their control. A series of German air raids on the United Kingdom started soon thereafter (IWM, 2018a). It was widely believed that families in the south and east of England were particularly vulnerable. In other cases, children were evacuated from regions where they had previously sought refuge in the wake of the disaster. Aerial dogfights involving British fighters and German bombers during the Battle of Britain were observed by many of those who stayed. The Home Guard was formed for the purpose of protecting towns and villages from an impending enemy invasion. Internment for children of Austrian or German origin is now a possibility. One hundred and fifty children were among the 14,000 Austrian and German nationals detained on the Isle of Man as "enemy aliens" during World War II.

Bombing Raids

The German air force began nighttime bombings of British cities in September 1940. First, London was bombed for 57 consecutive nights, followed by intense strikes on other major towns as the Blitz spread. 7,736 children were murdered during the Blitz and 7,622 were severely injured. A large number of youngsters had to deal with the loss of one or more siblings (IWM, 2018a). Both children and adults were affected by the bombing strikes. Adults, including Girl Guides and Boy Scouts, participated in air raid preparations (ARP), subsequently known as Civil Defense, by carrying messages, keeping watch over fires, or working with the volunteer services. They were all part of this effort. Many people lost their lives in the line of duty because of the inherent dangers of the job. There were new bombs and rockets, the V1 flying bomb and the V2 rocket, that wreaked havoc in 1944.

Homes During the Second World War

From decaying tenement slums to elegant mansions, British housing during World War II had a wide variety of standards. Outside lavatories and no bathrooms were still common in many households (IWM, 2018a). Children shared beds with their siblings or their parents in the past. Over 200,000 homes were completely destroyed by enemy bombs during World War II. This snapshot shows a prefabricated emergency house that many children had to relocate to many times. During the conflict, 34 million people had their addresses changed.

How Were Londoners Affected by Rationing and Shortages?

During the war, rationing was implemented to keep an eye on the flow of food and clothes. As fresh meat and fish became scarce, dried and canned food became more widespread. An initiative called "Dig for Victory" urged individuals to cultivate their own food to prevent fresh food shortages (Imperial War Museums, 2018). Farming occupied every possible acre of land. "Cabbage plants have taken their place in Kensington Gardens' flower beds"-All Londoners received coupon booklets like this one from the government. In order to accommodate children's growth spurts, the government provided them with an extra 66 vouchers every year. They rated everything. Five coupons were spent for shoes, but 18 coupons were utilized for a suit. To make their garments last longer, people were advised to make do and repair.

Different colored coupons decorated the book's pages. There are blue coupons to be found here. At any one moment, only one color was allowed to be utilized. To prevent individuals from using all of their coupons too soon, the government issued a schedule for when the next color might be utilized. This should have been the case, but it was not always the case with rationing (Imperial War Museums, 2018).

Is There a Reason Why Londoners Had to Wear ID Tags?

More than a million homes were damaged or destroyed during World War II. It is estimated that at least 80,000 Londoners were either killed or severely wounded in the attack. Children accounted for one out of every ten wartime fatalities. Injuries sustained by Londoners as a result of the bombings made it impossible to identify those who had been hurt. To expedite the procedure, police urged individuals to wear identification badges. Identification was made easier for Londoners by the widespread use of personalized metal bracelets like this one.

An id depicting Saint Christopher, patron saint of travelers, is fastened to this identification bracelet. This would have given wearers reassurance knowing they were safeguarded on their excursions.

How Did Londoners Protect Themselves?

During air attacks, many Londoners sought refuge in Anderson shelters, a kind of air-raid shelter. You can see what the interior of a shelter looked like in this etching. Sir John Anderson served as a government minister, and the shelters were named for him. Free shelters were supplied to any homeowners with a garden who made less than £250 per year by the government to use (Field, 2002). During the night, air attacks were more likely to occur. Families often stayed together in the shelter, as seen in the engraving. The shelter, which was six feet (almost two meters) high and buried in four feet (just over one meter) of dirt, was not always comfortable. Londoners, like those shown in the etching, lived in tight quarters with frequent flooding (Field, 2002).

It was only possible to utilize these shelters if you had a garden. Any accessible basement space, the Underground stations, or public surface shelters in open locations like parks were used by Londoners who didn't have a garden.

Experiences of a World War II Survivor During the Blitz

In 1940, Londoners were relieved when the feared invasion of Britain failed to materialize but soon faced a terrifying new menace. World War II veteran Joan McKenzie describes Hitler's V-weapons on-slaught during the Blitz, which she saw firsthand. Her story appeared in the April/May 1993 edition, when Joan MacKenzie described her life as a young woman working for Shell Oil near London during WWII. She spoke about the Blitz of 1940 and how the War forced her to "grow up quickly." Author John Wukovits continues her story in this issue.

After the war, MacKenzie remembers people saying, "My gosh, how near we came to an invasion!" (Wukovits, 2022). "And we had no chance of fending them off. We took down or redirected road signs and hid old farm equipment in fields to prevent aircraft from landing, but if the Germans had gained a foothold, we would have been doomed. But back then, I thought we were invincible. We had total faith in our leaders and were certain that we would triumph. There was never a time when people's spirits were down. In reality, Hitler's actions had the opposite impact. There was no way Hitler could beat us,' we would declare" (Wukovits, 2022).

Everywhere you walked,' MacKenzie recalls, "there were two buckets, one with sand and the other with water. For the safety of the roof, Shell Oil divided us into groups to keep an eye out for incendiaries that may set it ablaze. Buckets have been a part of our lives since we were children. The incendiary assaults on London were the most awful thing to behold," he said (Wukovits, 2022). "The sky was crimson, and you could smell the embers of the blazes. I walked through London one morning and noticed that the city's streets were littered with trash. Fires continued to flare on the outskirts of the city. Hoses were strewn over the ground, and the exhausted faces of the firefighters could be seen. Walked a distance that normally takes me 20 minutes in an hour" (Wukovits, 2022).

It's true that MacKenzie says, "We adjusted to any new thing that came along," including new weapons and food shortages. Despite the hardships caused by rationing, most individuals were able to get by. Raft cards were given to her mother so she could get what she needed (Wukovits, 2022). The item you were looking for was in one of the shops where you had an account and had been registered. Meat and vegetables were served in tiny amounts. There were hardly any eggs to be found. When I was a kid, I'd stare at an egg in my palm, trying to determine if I should scramble it, fry it, or bake it. To get what they needed, neighbors bartered excess goods with one another. Additional meat and extra veggies were brought in from the country to sell for cigarettes by MacKenzie's mother (Wukovits, 2022).

7

The Attacks on London—Story not Told

Some 30,000 people were killed and more than 51,000 were badly wounded in London as a result of German bombing raids. As aircraft technology advanced in the 1930s, the number of people who might be killed in a full-scale air war rose rapidly in the enormous metropolis. Some of their contemporaries predicted that a war might kill as many as 600,000 people in the United States, while military specialist Basil Liddell Hart predicted that 250,000 people would die or be wounded in the first week of a battle in 1939. With a belief that "the bomber would always get through," politicians and authorities hurried to build a civil defense as they envisaged societal disintegration, floods of refugees, and hospitals overwhelmed with people suffering from both physical and mental damage. "We must suppose that, under the strain of continuous assault on London, at least three or four million people will be forced out into the open country surrounding the capital," Churchill told the House of Commons in November 1934 (Field, 2002).

Reports from 1938 predicted that millions would be affected by varying degrees of neurosis and fear, according to the Ministry of Health's assessment. "London will be one giant raging bedlam, the hospitals will be assaulted, traffic will halt, the destitute will shout for aid" declared the Cambridge philosopher Bertrand Russell. Suddenly, it appeared possible to write apocalyptic science fiction stories. New York Mayor Rudolph Giuliani immediately noticed similarities in the Lon-

don Blitz, the German air campaign conducted against London between September 1940 and May 1941, after the horrific events of
September 11.

In the early press briefings at Ground Zero, he constantly contrasted
the courage and ingenuity of New Yorkers and Londoners, their ele-
vated feeling of community formed by risk, and the rise in patriotism
as a town and its inhabitants came to embody a country in peril (Field,
2002). Although the two circumstances couldn't be more unlike, his remarks struck a chord with me right away. Even though he was reading
John Lukacs' Five Days in London at the time, he was clearly thinking
about the city's reaction to the German invasion of France months before it was bombed to the ground. With Tony Blair's vocal backing for
the United States and quick (and solo) acceptance of unified military action, this conceptual coupling of London and New York was strengthened.

There was a deeper attraction to the historical analogy even if it was
flawed. Bush's speeches started to imitate Churchillian cadences soon after he began telling guests how much he admired Winston Churchill.
Karl Rove hung an image of Churchill in the Old Executive Office
Building, and the Oval Office now has a bronze bust of Churchill on
loan from the British government (Field, 2002). When it came to this
year's election, it seemed clear that Winston Churchill, a leader who
faced fascists and fanatics and ultimately prevailed, was the man for the
job. Certain "collective memories" (even if this does not necessitate any
thorough knowledge of the past) have particular resonance because of
the complicated reasons why certain historical narratives are given pref-
erence over others.

With its death camps and mass bombings, World War II changed
humanity's moral landscape and its destructive potential. It is generally
seen as both the 'hinge' on which much recent history spun and a struggle that redefined the moral landscape and mankind's destructive capacity. We have been so used to hearing about the war that its occurrence
after September 11 comes as no surprise. What's the point of going to

London to deal with this? A reference to a prior "Day of Infamy" would have conveyed impolitic anti-Japanese undertones even if the connection was more appropriate, for example, there was a minimal explicit mention of December 7, 1941. There are two other things to consider (Field, 2002). First and foremost, the bombing of London had a lasting impact because of the superb reporting of American journalists and broadcasters at the time, many of whom have now become household names.

The Nazis thought that because they had lost almost all of their friends, the United Kingdom would be open to negotiating a peace agreement with them. Because of their doubts about Germany's sincere desire for peace, the British government was adamantly opposed to a peace agreement. The Nazis stepped up their preparations for Operation Sealion, the secret name for the invasion of Britain, in the face of this resistance. The Nazis' first task was to annihilate the British Royal Air Force. Combat involving Luftwaffe fighters, German fighters, and British fighters was called the Battle of Britain because of this.

Londoners were taken completely by surprise on "Black Saturday." Luftwaffe planes flew over London late in the afternoon on a lovely day, as many residents were out enjoying it. The first sirens sounded at 16:43, the beginning of a 12-hour assault (White, 2016). At 05:00 on September 8, the "all clear" was sounded. There is no doubt that London was ravaged by one attack. 430 people were murdered and more than 1,600 were critically injured in the attack. Hospitals were unable to keep up. Winston Churchill visited the East End on September 8, where the attacks had been focused in order to destroy the docks, and he was impressed.

The Luftwaffe altered tactics in the subsequent attacks, which happened every day for two months without a pause. When it flew throughout the day on "Black Saturday," it came into contact with fighter aircraft from Fighter Command. After this, all assaults occurred at night, making it impossible for Fighter Command to intervene (White, 2016). When London was under attack on "Black Saturday," just 92 anti-aircraft guns were available to defend it. A massive upgrade to the city's defenses was ordered by Churchill soon after the outbreak of World War II. There were twice as many AA weapons in London within four days. In order to boost morale, the crews of these guns were told to fire at the invaders regardless of whether or not they could see them, since this created the idea that the defenders were doing a strong job.

The bombing of London's East End on August 24 and the following bombardment of Berlin on August 25 marked a watershed moment in the war. A wholesale bombardment of London was ordered by Göring, who had authorized the first strike. Bombing civilian targets became a regular occurrence as a result of this decision. The SC-50 bomb, which weighed 110 pounds and contained 55 pounds of TNT, was the favorite weapon of the Luftwaffe during the early days of the Blitz (NET, 2021). This many bombs could be carried by a Heinkel III. Even the tiniest particles of shrapnel flung off by the metallic shell were lethal, as metal shards flew at 7,000 mph during the first phases of the explosion.

People in London's shelters should have been protected from shrapnel, according to theory. But for individuals who volunteered to assist in the event of a terrorist attack, this was not the case. Known as "Blast Lungs," this was another cause of mortality. A bomb explosion caused a victim's lungs to rise up inside the rib cage, resulting in the lungs malfunctioning. The person died from suffocation, yet there were no evident physical injuries (NET, 2021). When the Luftwaffe began dropping more powerful bombs on London, the terror increased. TNT weighed 551 pounds on the SC-500. A Heinkel III could carry four ordinances of 500 pound TNT, similar to four SC-50s, a Heinkel III could carry four. They were capable of wreaking havoc (Trueman, 2022). To frighten Londoners into surrendering, the SC-500s were deployed in conjunction with incendiary bombs as the Blitz raged forth.

While the East End bombing attacks were devastating for London, they gave the RAF important time to recuperate from the strikes on their own runways and airports, despite the fact that they were destructive.

In reality, the number of fatalities caused by the Blitz was far fewer than the administration had anticipated. Research from 1938 anticipated that there would be up to two million fatalities, yet only 22,000 individuals had died. A variety of factors contributed to the low death tolls that the administration had hoped for. The Anderson shelters and the London Underground both saved numerous lives thanks to the shelter program. People who earned less than £250 a month were allowed to apply for a free Anderson shelter. More than three million Anderson shelters were distributed by the government. They provided excellent protection from falling bombs if they were constructed correctly.

The Chislehurst caverns in Kent provided a more secure and expansive haven for Londoners fleeing the city. By mid-October, as many as 15,000 individuals had taken sanctuary in the privately-owned buildings. However, the most significant community shelters were those located at the London Underground or Tube stations. Many people sought refuge there during World War I, but in 1939, the government rejected the idea of using them as refuges, citing the need for unhindered traffic flow for civilians and military personnel, as well as the danger of people developing a "deep shelter" mentality and refusing to leave their homes. It was enticing for more individuals to enter the Tube because of the frequency of the raids.

A few minor altercations erupted between the people gathered above and the Underground authorities tasked with locking the doors once the raid started, some of which were staged by Communist party supporters. It was only after the second week of intense bombardment that orderly lineups of passengers outside stations became a frequent sight, waiting for four PM when they were permitted to enter the platforms. On platforms, between the lines themselves, once the electricity was switched off, and propped up against escalator steps, they all sat or slept crowded together, as caught by the amazing images of Bill Brandt. When the bombings were bad enough, many families would take refuge in the Tube.

Around 150,000 people slept there every night in mid-September, but by winter and spring, that number had dropped to 100,000 or fewer (Trueman, 2022). There was a muted explosion of bombs and anti-aircraft barrages at deeper stations, but direct strikes on certain stations resulted in a serious loss of life (Marble Arch, Balham, Bank, Liverpool Street, etc). The Blitz had wreaked havoc on British towns by February 1941, but to Hitler's annoyance, the British people's morale remained strong. Thus, in order to force the nation into surrender, the Luftwaffe started bombing ports. Plymouth, Liverpool, and Belfast were among the cities targeted.

On May 8, 1941, a retaliatory attack was launched on Bremen and Hamburg in an effort to boost morale. Hitler launched one last big strike on London in retaliation for the raid. Hitler realized on September 14, 1940, that an invasion of the United Kingdom was out of the question. Operation Sealion was put on hold indefinitely. The Blitz, as the air raids on London came to be called, lasted until May 11, 1941 (Wikipedia, 2020). The Blitz came to an end shortly after this raid, when Hitler launched his invasion of the Soviet Union.

"It was the people of London who seized leadership..." started the Blitz on September 7, 1940. Many people, including women and children, sought refuge in the Underground stations. Over eighty years after the start of the Blitz, we examine how London's major public transportation system, the Underground, became a popular destination to seek refuge from the German bombing assault. In spite of this, the government was opposed to the Underground being used in this way. 'Little attention was given yesterday night to the request of the Ministries of Home Security and Transport urging the people to abstain from utilizing the London Tube stations as air-raid shelters unless in an absolute need,' according to an item in the Hartlepool Northern Daily Mail of September 20, 1940. Instead, Londoners of all socioeconomic backgrounds raced to Underground stations to escape the carnage taking on above ground. By the end of September, refuge on the Underground had become a popular option for commuters, according to the Daily Herald.

London's Underground stations are always full of individuals looking for a place to sleep. In order to have a good night's rest, a lot of them show up early in the evening with their sleeping bags packed and ready to go. Some residents of the suburbs and surrounding areas are among the group.

8

Churchill and Britain in WW2

On September 3, 1939, the United Kingdom declared war on Nazi Germany, Winston Churchill was named First Lord of the Admiralty. On May 10, 1940, he took over as Prime Minister from Neville Chamberlain, a position he maintained until July 26, 1945. Churchill, who had been out of politics for much of the 1930s, had led the charge for British re-armament in response to the increasing militarism in Nazi Germany. He supervised British participation in the Allies' war effort against the Axis forces as Prime Minister. The 1945 Dresden bombing has raised questions about whether Churchill was a successful wartime commander who played a significant role in safeguarding Europe's liberal democracy against Nazism. During the first part of the war, he was the most significant Allied commander (Kindy, 2020).

On May 10, 1940, Winston Churchill was sworn in as prime minister of the United Kingdom. "I felt...that all my prior existence had been simply a preparation for this hour and for this ordeal," he later wrote. When Churchill achieved his lifelong goal of becoming prime minister, Germany had just invaded France, Belgium, the Netherlands, and Luxembourg the day before. Britain has to undergo its most difficult test ever (Kindy, 2020). Churchill is most known for his leadership during the turbulent years of 1940–1941, which included the evacuation of the British population from Dunkirk, the Battle of Britain, and the Blitz. He played a critical role in uniting the country against Hitler. "The only man we have for this hour," as Labour MP Hugh Dalton put it, was

Churchill. People in Britain mostly agreed with this sentiment (Taylor, 2018).

In a less evident way, Churchill simplified and streamlined political and military planning and decision-making. The 'Big Three' Alliance, which included the United States, Russia, and the United Kingdom, was bolstered by his charisma. His boundless energy and ambition made it difficult to work with him on a regular basis. It's worth it, Field Marshal Sir Alan Brooke wrote, 'to have the opportunity of working with such a person. The Conservative Party lost a landslide win over Labour in the general election of July 1945, when Nazi Germany had been vanquished and Japan was on the verge of collapse. It was a war-weary electorate that was eagerly anticipating a new Britain. Once again, Winston Churchill, the man who had done so much to ensure the success of the Allies, was out of government.

Weapons of the Mind

Few genuine weapons were available to Churchill in the early stages of the Second World War. Instead of using violence, he used words. The remarks he made at that time are among the most impactful in English. Words that were bold, brave and human were punctuated by moments of lightheartedness. All of Nazi-occupied Europe and the rest of the globe were included in their outreach. "He grabbed the English language and sent it into combat," noted journalist Beverley Nichols (Taylor, 2018).

September 1939 to May 1940: First Lord of the Admiralty

The Fake War and the Norwegian Campaign

It was on this day in 1939 when Britain declared war on Germany that Chamberlain reappointed Winston Churchill to his post as First Lord of the Admiralty, a position he had held since the start of World War One. Chamberlain's war cabinet included him among its members as a result. Churchill subsequently claimed that the Board of Admiralty sent a signal to the Fleet upon learning of his appointment: "Winston is back." No proof for this narrative has been uncovered by Richard Langworth or Martin Gilbert, the official biographer of Winston Churchill, despite Lord Mountbatten repeating it in a 1966 address at Edmonton.

As First Lord, Churchill was one of the most prominent ministers during the so-called "Phoney War," when the only meaningful activity by British troops was on the oceans. Immediately after the Battle of the River Plate on December 13, 1939, Churchill was full of joy and greeted the sailors upon their return, praising them for "a superb sea combat" and adding that their deeds throughout the harsh, dark winter had "warmed the cockles of the British heart (Gilbert, 1991). Admiral Graf Spee had detained some 300 British soldiers, and on February 16, 1940, Winston Churchill personally ordered the destroyer HMS Cossack's Captain Philip Vian to seize the German supply ship Altmark on the Norwegian seas and free the detainees (Taylor, 2018). As a result of these acts and words, Churchill's reputation was greatly strengthened.

To counter the growing threat of German naval operations in the Baltic Sea, he considered sending a naval force there. However, he swiftly switched to a different strategy, code-named Operation Wilfred, to mine Norwegian waterways and block iron ore exports from Narvik to Germany (Shakespeare, 2018). Mining was a contentious issue, with the war cabinet and the French government both have a say. Thus, Wilfred had to wait until the day before the German invasion of Norway on April 8, 1940, before he could finally arrive.

The Battle on the Home Front

All Britons, including Churchill, had difficulties as a result of World War II. Both his son Randolph and daughter Mary enlisted in the Auxiliary Territorial Service and served in an anti-aircraft unit during World War II (Taylor, 2018). Children, including Churchill's grandson, were evacuated from British cities and other target locations to avoid German air attacks during World War II Occasionally, sympathetic Americans helped reduce British rationing and shortages during World War II.

Roosevelt—Churchill Awards

At a meeting in New York City on the first of 1942, Churchill and Roosevelt signed a proclamation that established the United Nations. Twenty-six nations finally joined this wartime alliance, which became the foundation of a long-lasting international organization. Churchill spent the next year focusing on improving ties with his most vital allies, the United States and the Soviet Union, as well as the Free French under the leadership of Charles de Gaulle (Taylor, 2018). When it came to grand strategy and the future of the British Empire, Churchill and Roosevelt had numerous disagreements, but they were able to work things out in face-to-face discussions in Washington and Casablanca.

Chamberlain's Resignation and the Norway Debate

A public discussion on the government's handling of the war was conducted in Parliament on May 7–9, after all the Allies had failed to prevent the German takeover of Norway. Known as the Norway Debate, it is widely regarded as one of the most momentous occurrences in the history of parliament. The Labour opposition asked for a vote of no confidence in Chamberlain's administration on the second day (Wednesday, May 8). Despite the fact that he was widely admired on both sides of the aisle, Churchill had to speak on behalf of the administration since he was a part of it. His job was put in jeopardy because of his need to protect the government while maintaining his personal reputation. Despite winning the election, the government's majority was substantially weakened by demands for the formation of a national government.

Germany attacked Belgium, Luxembourg, and the Netherlands in the early hours of May 10 as a precursor to their assault on France. Chamberlain had been seeking to build a coalition since the division vote, but on Friday afternoon, Labour said that they would not serve under his leadership, but would welcome another Conservative. There were just two candidates: Winston Churchill and Foreign Secretary Lord Halifax. Chamberlain, Halifax, Churchill, and the government's Chief Whip had previously met on the subject on the 9th to discuss it. Chamberlain recommended the King choose Churchill as prime minister after Halifax realized he could not manage successfully in the House of Lords. The first thing he did was to thank Chamberlain for his support by writing him a letter.

Churchill subsequently claimed that he felt relieved since he now had control over the whole situation. "A preparation for this hour and for this struggle," he said of his life, which he saw as him walking with destiny (Arthur, 2017).

A Well—Recognized Leader

Workers welcome Winston Churchill on his visit to bomb-damaged Plymouth on May 2, 1941. This was just one of several trips he made throughout the country to promote morale. Between July 1940 and May 1945, public opinion surveys were still in their infancy, yet they consistently found that 78% of those asked approved of Churchill as prime minister.

Reactions to Churchill's Appointment as Premier

At best, Churchill's entrance to the premiership was similar to a hasty wartime marriage. If any political party in the House of Commons did not win a majority, and he was appointed as an MP, then the House of Lords was entirely mute. Chamberlain was the head of the Conservative Party until he was forced to quit due to bad health in October. He died of cancer in November of that year. It was just a matter of time before Churchill became the new leader of the Conservative Party (Ingersoll, 1940, p. 127). In November, Ralph Ingersoll wrote in his column: "The enthusiasm, bravery, and focus of [Churchill] were praised wherever I visited in London. Many people expressed concern about the future of the United Kingdom without him. He was clearly well-liked.

After the war, no one expected him to be prime minister. He was just the right person at the right moment at the right place for the right reason. Currently, Britain is engaged in a desperate fight with its adversaries" (Ingersoll, 1940, p. 127).

Creation of the Ministry of War

At 65 years old, Winston Churchill became prime minister thanks to the war's revitalizing effects. Gunther said in 1940 that Churchill "looks 10 years younger than he is" and claimed that he was the only World War I commander remaining in a prominent political position (Gunther, 1919, pp. 328, 332–333). Knickerbocker said about this in 1941 "Now, more than any other human being, he must shoulder enormous duties. This weight should have a crushing impact on him, one would assume. Absolutely not. While the Battle of Britain was in full swing, he seemed to be twenty years younger than he had been before the conflict. People are inspired by his positive outlook nonetheless.

Five-man war cabinet: Chamberlain as Lord President of the Council, Attlee as Lord Privy Seal (later Deputy Prime Minister), Halifax as Foreign Secretary, and Arthur Greenwood, Labour's Arthur Greenwood without a portfolio. On a regular basis, service heads and ministers would join these five during meetings. As the conflict proceeded, the size and composition of the cabinet altered.

Churchill, Attlee, and Greenwood were joined by Ernest Bevin as Minister of Labour and National Service; Anthony Eden as Foreign Secretary; Lord Beaverbrook as Minister of Aircraft Production; Sir Kingsley Wood as Chancellor of Exchequer; and Sir John Anderson as Lord President of the Council—replacing Chamberlain, who died in No. 8 Squadron. With this combination, Jenkins characterized it as being a "war cabinet for winning" in contrast to Chamberlain's "war cabinet for losing." With the establishment of the job of Defense Minister, Churchill became the most powerful British prime minister during World War II in response to concerns that there had been no apparent single minister in control of the prosecution of the war.

It was important for Churchill to have colleagues he knew and trusted in government. Frederick Lindemann was a personal friend of Beaverbrook and served as the government's scientific adviser at this time. One of several 'technocrats' brought in from the outside, Lindemann played an important role, notably on the home front. He would be happy to say that his administration was the most inclusive in British political history because it included persons like Lord Lloyd, who was on the extreme right, and Ellen Wilkinson, who was on the far left.

Achievement and Failure

The last year of the war was both a period of immense victory and a moment of deep despair for Winston Churchill. By the end of July 1944, Allied ground troops had broken through enemy lines and were threatening Germany itself. The Battle of the Bulge, a Nazi counteroffensive, proved to be merely a short setback, and the conclusion of the war seemed clear at the time. However, as Soviet soldiers moved across Eastern Europe and the Balkans, imposing communism in their path, looming postwar issues cast a shadow on the imminent victory. Franklin Roosevelt and Adolf Hitler, two of Churchill's greatest adversaries during World War II, both died in April 1945. The conflict in Europe came to an end the next month with the signing of the Armistice. But he heard of his own political loss at the last wartime conference in Potsdam, Germany when the British public voted him and his Conservative Party out of power (Shakespeare, 2018).

9

From the Ones Who Survived

The Blitz period was devastating for every person who lived through
it. Many lost their loved ones or were separated from them. Mass
evacuations happened, and children were sent far away from their
homeland. When the Blitz started, people sought shelters in the underground stations. They got jammed, and fires were all over the place. In
some cases, bombs were dropped on the refuge, creating mass havoc in
Britain. Families were dug out of the debris, and some even found unexploded bombs in their gardens. People experienced a rough time during
the war. Those who survived can never forget the horror of the London
Blitz. Hence, here we bring you ten survivors who recount their inci-
dents from the Blitz.

Joan McKenzie

Joan McKenzie gracefully survived Hitler's invasion of Britain. She
used to work as a Shell Oil employee near London when the Blitz took
its origin. She describes that World War II made her grow up fast.
McKenzie recalls that England was very close to a German invasion.
England would not have been able to put much resistance if the Nazis
had acquired a foothold on the land. Road signs were either uprooted
or turned the wrong way; farmers had to put their old machinery on
their farms so that German planes did not have a place to land. McKenzie used to think that Britain was invincible. She believed what the leaders at that time told them.

McKenzie remembers that the German bombers bombed almost every large city in England. She describes that at least two buckets filled with water and sand could be found anywhere you went. She even possesses a picture of her friend's wedding. Behind her in that photo, two buckets could be easily spotted. The volatile attacks on London changed the sky's color into red. One could easily sense the ashes igniting. She believes that people adapted to the new changes brought along by WWII. Rationing of food and clothes was imposed on people. Even McKenzie's mother got one. She would usually get small amounts of meat, fruits, and vegetables. Eggs were a luxury for the people in England during the Blitz. She used to get confused about how the elegant eggs are to be used—scrambling, frying, or using it for baking food.

The neighborhood would trade surplus items to fulfill their needs. For instance, McKenzie's mother acquired additional meat. People from the countryside would come with vegetables to exchange them for cigarettes. She recalls that even the water was rationed. People had to draw a line on their bathtub, which usually was up to five inches. She maintains a good relationship with her memories of the Blitz. She believes that war had its benefits as it brought many people together. At last, she says, "Mostly, I remember the good times, not the sad" (Wukovits, 2022).

Pensioner Mary

Pensioner Mary has a rather vivid memory of the Blitz. Blitz happened when she was just a teenager. Her mother used to be away fruit-picking; her siblings migrated due to the danger posed by WWII. Only Mary and her sister lived in the family house. The day appeared when she was waiting for her aunt on the street. Luftwaffe started bombing; all the terraced homes were eaten by the bombs. Mary couldn't withstand the scenes and was heavily moved. Tears started pouring from her eyes. Suddenly, she saw her sister coming from her friend's house. She just said, "Mary." Both of them ran toward each other; it was just like a film. Luckily, both Mary and her sister survived the Blitz.

Roy

Most pensioners remember near-miss encounters with the bombs. Well, Roy's experience was a tragic incident. He was a schoolboy when the Blitz happened. He remembers sleeping in a school with his dad while the other family members migrated amidst war. Roy describes that his family was chilling when the sirens blew off. His grandad was making cocoa for all the members in the kitchen. When the explosion happened, the Roy family was filled with terror. They could listen to the havoc created by the bombers. They could not hear any help signals from the grandad. They had to spend several hours within the partially crushed house. Roy remembers that his mum and gran looked like ghosts covered in sand and dust. Luckily, someone came to help them as the explosions got quieter. People would violently tug the tumbled door, and finally, they could see a beam of light that led to a path of safety. Roy was forced to go into a saddened stage due to the destruction of his home. Windows were all shattered, beds were dangling through the roof, water pouring all over, and the ominous sound of sizzle gas was depressing to see.

Roy recalls that they were transported to the nearest hospital for treatment. Unfortunately, their grandad was killed when the bombing started (Chelsea Pensioners, 2020).

Julia Draper

Julia Draper was a British Red Cross nurse when the Blitz happened. Julia was married to her first husband in 1939, who worked as one of President Eisenhower's aides at the British embassy. She describes him as a wonderful man who had a significant influence over people. Unfortunately, he died due to a plane crash when coming back from North Africa. During the Blitz, it is safe to say that she tried to keep a semblance of regular life. She describes that while her time in Camberley, Surrey as a nurse, they had organized many parties, theater plays, pictures, etc. Young people met and had romances in a more carefree manner as nobody knew whether they would see tomorrow or not. Following orders wasn't a primary goal for the people living in Surrey, but they still tried to.

She further mentions that Camberley was attacked numerous times by the Luftwaffe. But thankfully, she was not close to the bomb-affected region. People maintained their bold and resilient spirit to serve the country. She even appeared in the famous British magazine *Tatler*. She explains that people were horrified in London as they were in constant danger of being bombed. When the Blitz concluded, she remarked, "We could finally breathe" (Jewsbury, 2010).

Betty Popkiss

Betty Popkiss was a brave girl in her teenage years. She had just left schooling when the Blitz happened. At that time, she had joined the St. John Ambulance in Coventry. She dug out a family after their Anderson shelters got devoured by the bombings. For this action, she also won a George medal on October 19. She conveys that the Blitz had showered horror among the people of Britain. When the bombings began, she had just become a volunteer for St. John Ambulance. That night, Betty called the air precautions post located in Hen Lane, Holbrooks. She had the advantage that her posting was close to where she lived. Hence, she used to call the air precautions department on most dusks to know what was happening in England.

The Luftwaffe announced their arrival with a shower of slow-burning incendiaries. People were running to find shelter for themselves. One of the males ran up to Betty and told her that his house's roof was getting fumed. He anxiously asked her if they could get a ladder so that Betty would stop the home from catching fire. She exclaimed that she hated heights. Hence, she was a bit nervous, but both showed brave characteristics. They were able to eradicate flames with a bucket and stirrup pump. As she was walking home, the atmosphere grew darker. The Luftwaffe warriors had started the main shelling; sirens were screaming all over. The anti-aircraft guns of Britain were smoldering as the bombers were pouring heavy explosives. A little girl abruptly arrived in front of Betty, and she just said three words: "Mummy, Daddy... please..." She could sense that something terrible had happened. She directed the little girl to run to the ARP post to call for help while she ran through the damaged road.

She noticed that an Anderson shelter made a nearly direct impact with a bomb. As she approached the damaged house, she discovered her neighbors were trapped inside the debris. Intuitively, she began unearthing the ruins with her bare hands. It was not enough to rescue the entangled neighbors. She needed something to uplift the debris; remarkably, she found a spade nearby. The frightening part was that there was no shouting and screaming from inside; it was just whining. Luckily, a boy arrived in his vehicle near the street. Betty glanced up and detected that the door directing to the kitchen had been blown open. She shouted at the young boy, "go upstairs and get some blankets." She could clearly tell that he didn't want to go upstairs. He was frightened. She pushed him to do the job while other people arrived to help Betty free her neighbors. They all diligently worked hard to rescue the trapped people. The only light source they had during the time was from the shells blasting overhead.

Finally, seven members of the trapped family were rescued and Betty helped them with first aid. She even took out her brand new black coat and spread it over them. For this bravery act, she got the George Medal.

Jimmy Fraser

Jimmy Fraser had worked all his life as a chiefship draftsman at the shipyard in Aberdeen. He had a tragic experience at the Blitz because he was almost devoured by a Luftwaffe bomb. He describes that he was only 18 when the Blitz started and worked as a shipyard apprentice. We all know that ports and shipyards were prominent targets of the German bombers. Hence, one day, when Fraser was in the drawing office, a bomb descended on the yard just before lunchtime. Fraser and his office mates were on the top floor when this incident happened.

When they were on their way to the shelter, a bomb dropped right across the refuge. He exclaimed that they were lucky enough to not get close to the cover. Otherwise, they would have been brutally killed by the bomb. Many nearby boiler shops were destroyed, and the people who sought refuge in the shelters were all massacred. To add to his misery, Fraser had another encounter with the bombs. He was employed as an Air Raid Precautions messenger at a fish market. On one of the nights, the Luftwaffe dropped another bomb in the pub across the ARP station. Well, his luck overpowered the Luftwaffe bombs. He survived the attack. He described, "When I came out, there was just a white cloud of smoke left."

Reginald Willis

Reginald Willis was hired at an airdrome as a rigger. Unfortunately, he worked at the epicenter of the Blitz, South London. Just like Fraser, he experienced a near-miss with the bombs. He conveys that he was 21 when the Blitz started. He worked in the support team at the Kenley Airdrome. Reginald was this close to being killed by the bomb that went across the street where he lived. According to Reginald, he was courting his wife at that time. He described that he had frequently visited her during the time because he had to meet one of his friends at Thornton Heath Ponds.

The bomb did not shatter the house's window, but it flew toward him. Even though he was left stunned by the incident, he wasn't afraid. He says that he doesn't remember the blast that clearly. But the shrapnel bombs and the metal that flew toward him developed a lasting effect on his mind.

Jean Savill

Jean Savill was a child when the Blitz happened. She used to live in Lewisham but got evacuated due to a series of air raids, along with the two neighbor's children. Before she got rescued, a bomb had fallen over her house's garden. Luckily, it didn't blow up. She explains that her sister was the one who found the bomb. They had an outside toilet, and just beside it, a bomb was lying quietly. It was startling for the Savill family. Hence, they called for help, and two wardens responded to the plea with a barrow and shovel. They carefully dragged the bomb away from the house. She says that she doesn't remember the horrible things about the Blitz, such as the rockets or bombs. Although, she does remember the window being blown in on her during the raid. This was also the reason that she migrated to a safer home.

She quite liked the shelter located near the end of a street in Lewisham. There was constant singing in the refuge area, which she enjoyed. When she came home after the Blitz ended, she could only see that everything had been bombed in Lewisham.

Ron Leagas

Ron Leagas had a unique experience with the Blitz. Similar to Reginald, he lived in London. Ron had to go through at least five or six raids before entering the British Army. One night, he was roaming outside when the sirens blew off. Everyone ran towards the underground shelters at Clapham Common, which gave refuge to at least 1,000 people. All people were crammed into the tunnel, and the situation became horrendous. The atmosphere became cold quickly. It was damp and smelly and consisted of metal beds that were uncomfortable to sleep on.

He conveys that the people didn't have any choice but to seek shelter in those congested areas. The situations were worse outside, and if any warden found you on the street, they'd eventually throw you inside. He remembers those times as the worst stage of his life. One of those nights, the German bombers had dropped two bombs into the cemetery across the street. The amount of mess created by them was unimaginable. Decomposed bodies and skeletons could be found everywhere, whether in parks or streets. People picked them up and reburied them in the cemetery. The scenes weren't pleasant for anyone, but it was necessary to be completed.

June Wilson

June Wilson was one of those who migrated amidst the Blitz. First, she got evacuated to Hove and then to Peaslake in Surrey. Although, she got homesick and was returned to her homeland in South Norwood. She explains that the first year of World War II was relatively quieter. Hence, her parents would take her back home in September 1940. After she came back, the Blitz started. There were air raids, bombs, everywhere. But now, there was no turning back for June Wilson. Hence, she stayed with her parents and went to a school in Croydon. Sirens would go off constantly, and attack guns would try to shoot the Luftwaffe planes down. The scenes were horrific for June Wilson and her family. They would hear the sounds of explosions constantly.

June's dad worked as a bus driver. Hence, he had to drive to most parts of London, and fortunately, no bombs got dropped along his route. June continually remained worried about her dad due to his profession during the Blitz.

David Varlow

David Varlow was just six months old when the Blitz happened. Although, now he is a retired police officer living in Kent. He began searching for his twin brother, who got disconnected from him due to an air raid in Southsea in Portsmouth. Due to his minor age, he does not remember what happened during the time. His mother was blessed with twins. When the night of the bombs arrived, his mother was on her way to the shelter. She was afraid that she would not make it to the refuge center. Hence, she gave his brother, Richard, to a nun. Unfortunately, the nun disappeared after the incident. He assumes that the nun took shelter in the same one where he and his mother did.

David says that his mother told this story when he was seven. But couldn't verify more about the situation due to his mother's death when he was 13. He started looking for his brother by making inquiries in Portsmouth. Unfortunately, he couldn't even find his brother's birth or death certificate. There should have been one, but he assumes that it may have been destroyed due to the Blitz (Independent, 2010).

Chapter 10: Stories of the Brave

We all know about the mass destruction showered on Britain by the Luftwaffe. The destruction and casualties caused due to it were unimaginable. Hence, there was a need for people to step up and help the threatened people. In response to the Blitz, many people showed their courage during the civilian attacks in 1940. A new gallantry medal was created to award these great men and women. Named after King George VI, the George Cross (GC) rewarded those who displayed brave acts away from the battle heat. GC is considered an equivalent to the Victoria Cross, which rewards the soldiers who show extreme bravery on the battlefield. Initial awards were primarily given to those involved in rescue work and bomb disposal. Those who knew that their life was endangered but still went to save other people are the worthy owners of the George Cross.

Extraordinary Heroes at IWM London

The stories of the 10 men listed below are full of bravery and courage. All these men earned the George Cross honor while helping others during the Blitz. IWM London showcases their awards in the Lord Ashcroft Gallery.

Bennett Southwell GC

Benett Southwell was just a month into his work as a bomb disposer when the day of devastation arrived. That day, a German mine had fallen over a house in Shoreditch. The day this incident happened was the October 19, 1940. The catch was that the bomb had failed to explode. Benett and his commanding officer, Sub Lieutenant Jack Easton, went to the cited location. The people in that region had been vacated. Apparently, the bomb's rest position was a bit awkward. Hence, Easton determined to defuse the bomb at its resting position without disturbing it. Southwell helped by giving him the tools required. Suddenly, the bomb started ticking, which is the worst nightmare for anyone working on a bomb.

It was clear that they only had 12 seconds to run and hide in a safe place. Southwell headed down the road, whereas Easton plunged for shelter. The mine exploded with full force, causing destruction in all the nearby houses. Unfortunately, Southwell was captured at the scene and died on the spot. Easton was lucky enough to survive the blast. The George Cross was awarded to Benett Southwell and Jack Easton for their bravery. Marion, the wife of Benett Southwell, posthumously received the GC from King George VI at Buckingham Palace in October 1941.

John Babington GC

Being from a scientific background, John Babington had an interest in Physics. He even worked as a sub-lieutenant in the Royal Naval Volunteer Reserve. During World War II, he operated in the bomb disposal unit. The man was calm and composed, always thought before doing any action, and had good skills in the high-risk job of bomb disposal. Luckily, he endured the battle and went back to teaching science. Jon Babington died in 1992 after doing heroic acts in the Second World War.

John Babington experienced a tense situation in the late 1940s. A German mine had anchored in the Chatham Dockyard of Kent, unexploded. The sheer size of the mine had made a 16-foot-deep pit on the ground. The mine was a new variation, meaning that it came with a new kind of anti-handling fuse. An RAF soldier had died a few weeks earlier while trying to defuse the same bomb. Hence, it had a dangerous potential of exploding. Even with the magnitude of the danger, Sub Lieutenant John Babington went to defuse the mine.

Babington had to attach a line to the head of the fuse in an attempt to remove it. For three continuous instances, the cable broke. Although the mine could have detonated at any moment, still he went down the pit. At last, Babington was successful in his mission, and the bomb was cautiously raised up and eliminated. His bravery led him to receive the GC award. It even assisted the bomb disposal authority to understand how to deal with these new devices.

Robert Davies GC

September 12, 1940, was the night of heavy raids in London. Several bombs were dropped, but one of them landed almost beneath St Paul's Cathedral. An officer of Royal Engineers named Lieutenant Robert Davies was sent to deal with the unexploded havoc. Due to its heavy mass, the bomb made a pit of 26 feet (eight meters). Davies faced a problem; he could neither detonate nor disarm the bomb. Detonating would mean destroying the cathedral too. The only viable way was to remove it undamaged. It was a life-threatening task for Davies and his men. It took them around three days to remove the bomb without exploding it. The Blitz had made the London streets completely unable to operate. The electrical cables were damaged, and gas mains were ruptured. All these conditions made the operation more dangerous.

After the bomb got excavated, it was necessary to dispose of it. Hence, Davies took this responsibility because he desired to save his men from further danger. He took the wheel and drove it to Hackney Marshes in East London as it was the closest cemetery for bombs. Hence, at the center of the Marshes, Davies discharged the bomb, leaving a 30-meter-wide crater. Robert Davies and his men were named the "bomb squad" that saved St Paul's cathedral. If it had been destroyed, the British morale would have gotten crushed as it is an important London landmark. For this act, Davies acquired the George Cross honor in September 1940.

Brandon Moss GC

As Coventry is a vital city in England, it mourned a lot during the Blitz. The night of November 14 and 15, 1940, was devastating for Coventry and its citizens. German bombers continued their air raids for 11 continuous hours. Brandon Moss was one of the soldiers deployed in Coventry that night. Being a Special Constable during WWII, he served in the defense forces for the most part. Due to his high-risk job, he had to evade death several times. The night raid destroyed several houses, and a wrecked bus stood in a depressing scene. Moss knew that three people were trapped inside the wrecked bus. Hence, he had to lead a rescue operation in fatal conditions that included crumbling debris and gas leaks. His motive was to clear a tunnel for the trapped people so that they could escape. Seeing the devastating situation, many rescuers gave up. But Moss was determined; he kept moving forward. Actions paid off, and Moss was able to free all three people.

This was not the end of his operation, as more people were entangled in the neighboring house. Helping them would again mean risking his own life. But still, he went to save people while also battling his exhausted body. His superhuman efforts lasted from 11:00 PM to 6:30 AM that night. Brandon Moss became the first Special Constable honored with a George Cross. He continued saving people for the rest of the war and retired from his job in 1948.

Selby Armitage GC

Selby Armitage was a skillful bomb disposer. He was an official in the Royal Naval Volunteer Reserve and was called for war in 1939. For his studies, Selby went to a mining school in Portsmouth. He had his skills nurtured at HMS Vernon, the Royal Navy's torpedo. After some lessons and demonstrations, he became an expert in defusing bombs. This is also the reason he was called during the Blitz in 1940 to tackle the parachute mines. Parachute mines had a habit of landing at the most awkward places. Once, Armitage had to deal with a bomb that had landed on the top of a factory. Another bomb was dangling on a tree in Orpington, Kent. The only way to reach there was through an unsteady ladder. One mistake would have the bomb ticking, and Armitage wouldn't have a chance to run. He stayed calm and composed and successfully defused the parachute mine. Once the bomb he was defusing started to tick. Armitage could only sprint 82 feet (25 meters) before it blasted. Even though he barely survived, his sheer determination allowed him to rejoin his work the next day. He was a part of those eight people who received the George Cross and George Medal for their heroic acts.

Reginald Ellingworth GC

Reginald Ellingworth was one of those who served in World War I and World War II. In WWI, he served in the Royal Navy, whereas he worked as a torpedo specialist in the Second World War. Eventually, he joined the Rendering Mines Safe team, where he operated closely with Lieutenant-Commander Richard Ryan. This pair specialized in tackling unexploded magnetic mines. The work could prove fatal anytime, precisely when the workers made one minor mistake. The day of September 21, 1940 was tiring for both Ellingworth and Ryan as they had defused several mines that day. That day, they were called to Dagenham, East London, to deal with the German mine. That bomb was found hanging on the roof of a cottage located in a densely-populated province. Ellingworth and Ryan weren't scared of the danger. Hence, they marched toward the bomb to make it safe. While doing so, the bomb suddenly exploded, devouring both men. For their bravery, both of them received the posthumous George Cross.

Harold Newgass GC

The Royal Naval Volunteer Reserve recruited Harold Newgass during the initial period of WWII. Harold volunteered to join the bomb disposal unit because he had never gone to sea. By the time Blitz started, Newgass had become an expert in defusing the unexploded German parachute mines. The night of November 28, 1940 saw a devastating air raid on Liverpool by the Luftwaffe. One of the dropped bombs landed unexploded on the roof of a gasholder in Garston, Merseyside. A bigger problem was that the gasholder possessed at least 2 million cubic feet of gas, implying that the gas reserve for half of Liverpool was endangered. The gas industry became paralyzed, the surrounding region reached a deadlock, and at least 6,000 people were evacuated.

Before dealing with the bomb, 1.25 million gallons of water had to be drained out of the gasometer. Hence, the officers started preparations for the operation, but it was evident that the mission was life-threatening. Even though Harold Newgass knew that the process may take his life, he was determined to defuse the mine. The operation started on December 3. Harold wore an oxygen cylinder due to the contagious air inside the gasholder. Each cylinder was filled with oxygen that would last for 30 minutes. Harold would meet his demise if the mine started to tick because he would not have enough time to escape its wrath.

In his six trips to the gasholder, he would assess the situation and plan his approach accordingly. He would take the necessary equipment, place sandbags around the mine, and lash it securely. These decisions allowed him to reach the fuse of the mine. On his last trip to the gasholder, he finally defused the bomb. This act is a perfect embodiment of bravery and endurance. Newgass successfully kept the people of Liverpool safe and helped the industry to operate again. For this act, he received the George Cross honor in March 1941.

Michael Gibson GC

Sergeant Micheal Gibson was a part of the Royal Engineers when Second World War showered its terror on humanity. He was assigned to the No. 9 Bomb Disposal Company, with its base in Birmingham. Sergeant Gibson had to tackle various unexploded mines that had dropped across the West Midlands. His heroic incident happened on September 14, 1940 when Luftwaffe initiated a raid on Coventry, leaving two unexploded bombs in a factory. Dealing with those bombs was necessary. Hence, Sergeant Micheal Gibson and other members were appointed to defuse the bomb. Although one of the devices exploded, no one got injured. Now, Gibson's primary target was to locate the second bomb and defuse it. Unexpectedly, an unusual hissing noise was heard by the team. Anyone could predict that the bomb would explode at any second.

Gibson was fully aware of the danger. Still, he sent his team to a safe place and went to the bomb alone. Somehow, he was successful in extracting the fuse. Finally, the bomb was taken out of the factory and disposed of, thus, saving thousands of lives. For his bravery displayed on September 14, Sergeant Michael Gibson received the George Cross honor. Gibson had to go on another mission a month after this incident when the Luftwaffe launched another air raid on Coventry. He was accompanied by six bomb disposal men. This time, their job was to defuse a 550-lb bomb. They successfully transported it to the bomb cemetery, but it exploded as soon as they started to unload it, which killed all of them.

Francis Brooke—Smith GC

Francis Brooke-Smith was an active soldier in the merchant navy and the Royal Naval Reserve before WWII. By 1940, he became a sub-lieutenant and volunteered for the mine disposal work. He traveled all around Britain, defusing German parachute mines. December 1940 saw a mine tumble over the deck of a fire float in Manchester Ship Canal. As mentioned before, parachute mines had a bad habit of landing in awkward positions. This case was no different as the bomb landed near an engine, in a way that it became difficult for Francis to reach it. Francis lifted the mine from its place in his attempt to defuse it. It did help, but he ended up in an uncomfortable position to work on the device. As soon as he began his work, the fuse clock started to buzz.

Brook-Smith was a calm and composed man. He maintained his calm and tried to prevent the mine from detonating. The bomb's position was tricky, meaning that he barely could reach it and had to work with an unfamiliar new piece of equipment. Due to his sheer determination and concentration, Francis finally stopped the clockwork. He even prevented a highly unstable mine from detonating in East London just a month after this incident. Francis Brooke-Smith defused a total of 16 parachute mines in WWII. He even received the George Cross for his work as a bomb disposer.

Arthur Merriman GC

Arthur Merriman had a significant interest in science as he served most of his life as a science teacher. His profession was put to good use during WWII. When the war broke out, he began serving as an Assistant Director of Bomb Disposal with the Directorate of Scientific Research. He was promoted to be the Joint Secretary of the Unexploded Bomb Committee. His work included a significant amount of research on bombs and mines. When the Blitz started, he had to go around the country to deal with those parachute mines. He would often go undercover to do his job by fabricating a story. He would make believe that he was an air inspector. But in reality, his work was far more dangerous.

In the initial hours of September 11, 1940, London's Regent Street was given a 550-lb bomb by the German Bombers. Although, it landed without exploding. Hence, everyone was evacuated from the area, and then, Arthur Merriman entered the scene. He had to deal with an already ticking bomb, meaning that he had to race with the clock to make it safe. He started the operation by removing the highly explosive material from the interior of the bomb. Although, the bomb still possessed its explosive properties. Since the clock was ticking, Merriman started to work more quickly.

His scientific knowledge helped him to assume the explosion time of the bomb. When he felt that the bomb had become safer, he withdrew himself from the site. Shortly afterward, the bomb blasted. A situation where mass casualties and destruction would have happened was reduced to an explosion that caused only the shattering of nearby windows. It was all thanks to Merriman's efforts and calm nature. For saving London's West End from destruction, Arthur Merriman received the George Cross honor. Later, he was transferred to the Royal Engineers unit. His technical knowledge and expert advice helped in defusing bombs at many locations. Arthur did survive the war and died in the year 1972 (*10 Incredible Stories of Bravery during the Blitz*, n.d.).

10

Evidence of the London Blitz at Presen

Those who lived in London during the Blitz may still see the impact of the war in the city's rebuilt buildings, some of which have been restored to their former glory, while others have been repurposed. Visitors who want to learn about London's worst period will find the evidence of destruction less obvious. If you know where to look, a trip through downtown London might still show the wounds left behind by those days (Aceto, 2009). The Imperial War Museum is an excellent resource for learning about the Blitz and the city of London as a whole. There are really five museums at the IWM, but we're going to the drab main building on the south side of the Thames. In the museum's World War II display, "The Blitz Experience," an interactive exhibit, gives visitors a sense of the historical period, although one that is devoid of the harsh dread.

Their small group of tourists is led by a guide dressed as an air raid warden through a bombed-out London street by a guide in the role of an air raid warden. In this video, he warns us about the hazards of gas leaks and unexploded munitions. Despite the United States' then-neutral attitude, our guide reminds us that a percentage of the supplies originate from the United States as we pass a "spot of tea" truck (Aceto, 2009). With the sounds of rescue and oncoming bombers, the 'experience' is like negotiating a full-sized diorama. You may get a feel of the turmoil caused by the night raids and of life in London during the Blitz, despite the fact that it's dark and difficult to see at times.

This is where Winston Churchill and his war cabinet convened for a more exclusive look of wartime London. On the other side of the Thames, beneath what is now the Treasury Building, is the subterranean warren of primarily tiny, cramped chambers. It is just a short walk from Parliament and Westminster Abbey (Aceto, 2009). The bunker-like entryway, although not unique to the war, leads to the complex of chambers where some 115 sessions of the War Cabinet were held during the course of the conflict. In spite of the absence of Churchill's cigar smoke, his residence has been restored and it seems like September 1940 all over again.

The Map Room is where I'm most moved. This room has a gigantic map on one wall, and if you look closely, you'll notice thousands of small holes that formerly served as pushpins to mark the hundreds of convoys that provided Great Britain with its logistical lifeline, creating a massive, arcing curve over the Atlantic Ocean. An unassuming brick wall on a nondescript side street on Lord North Street, a few streets south, is another powerful visual image of the time that is all the more moving because of its position. In that spot, you can still see a giant 'S' stenciled on the wall, with an arrow pointing to one of the numerous air raid shelters the city formerly had. On the other side of the street, a wall-mounted sign identifies the location of a bomb shelter where Londoners might shelter during an airstrike. You'll see more of them if you keep your eyes peeled throughout town.

North of the Strand, the famed great road that extends from Trafalgar Square and turns into Fleet Street, we come across more impressive walls. The church of St. Clement Danes may be found in the center of the street. An important part of London's Danish population has worshiped here since the late eighth century (Aceto, 2009). The 1681 construction of Christopher Wren's English Renaissance-style structure is the third church to occupy the site. It was destroyed by German bombers on the night of May 10, 1941, the last and deadliest strike of the Blitz. But even though it has subsequently undergone extensive restoration, its walls still display significant wounds inflicted by the assault.

Other churches were not as fortunate. With St. Paul's Cathedral as a backdrop, the defiantly shining dome of Christ Church Greyfriars stands as a symbol of British resistance ever since it was taken during the Blitz. It was another Wren creation that is now little more than a wreck. This piece of stone wall is all that remains, with a repaired spire that was installed in 1960. Pews formerly existed, but now rosebushes have taken their place, a stark warning of St. Paul's potential demise.

The second kind of monument may be seen along the Thames embankment on the north side. Bas-relief brass sculpture representing the Blitz and RAF aircrews rushing for their aircraft may be seen at the Battle of Britain Monument, a low set of walls. The names of the hundreds of pilots and crew members who perished in the conflict are commemorated on memorial plaques. The memorial in the bottom corner mentions the nine Americans who joined the war, as well as the Czech and Polish pilots that flew for Britain and were important in the skies that summer. To me, the city of London is a monument itself, a witness to the spirit of the people of London to endure, persevere, and return the fight to the enemy in order to triumph.

Do what many Londoners, and even American airmen, did after a bombing: go to the local pub and order up a pint and some substantial fare. We've narrowed our search to one at the end of a little lane named Rose Street in the bustling neighborhood of Covent Garden in central London. The Lamb and Flag proudly displays a sign inside the establishment that claims the pub has been open since Elizabeth I's reign, excluding an air attack. Tommies with tin hats and buckled shoes and ruffled shirts must have had a pint here, I think, as I glance about this structure that seems like it's been here for ages-and before them, men in buckled shoes and ruffled shirts. In a structure that seems to have witnessed every chapter in the long history of a great city, what better place to contemplate one of its most significant moments?

In addition to being easily accessible on foot, London's world-famous underground system makes even greater distances a walkable experience. A pre-purchased Oyster card simplifies and reduces the cost of that journey; you may add to the card's value as needed. Even if you just have a few hours to spend at the museum, the main IWM London building is definitely worth the trip. The structure originally housed Bethlem Royal Hospital, better known as Bedlam, a notorious institution.

Entering the lobby, you'll see tanks from World Wars past, as well as the V-2 rocket and a battle-damaged German Panther tank. A Spitfire from the Battle of Britain, as well as P-51 Mustangs and Fw 190 fighter planes as well as an old V-1 flying bomb, may be seen frozen in mid-flight. For additional information on life in London during the Blitz, visit the Home Front area of the World War II exhibition, and don't miss the Morrison indoor bomb shelter, which is a wire box with a reinforced steel frame just large enough to contain several persons laying down (*Examples of Bomb Damage Still Seen Today*, n.d.). A total of more than 500,000 were given out free of charge during the Second World War. Admission to the museum is free, however, certain special exhibits require a fee.

Conclusion

How did the Londoners live in the catastrophic times of the Second World War? For the most part, Londoners spent their time living regular lives. Although their everyday lives were disrupted by the Nazis. For Londoners, there was no such thing as 'Good nights' during the Blitz. There were only bad nights, worst nights, and better nights.

Life was terrifying, particularly in London because it was the main target of the German bombers. No person that lived near the targeted cities could sleep easily. Sometimes, the Luftwaffe would make mistakes and drop the bombs in entirely wrong areas. At other times, they would drop the leftover bombs at random. It increased the hardships of the Londoners as they didn't know when a bomb would fall on them. The most affected region was the Kent countryside. It came to be known as 'bomb alley' since it was located on the flight path to London. The bombing caused mass destruction, fear, death, and injury. Many families were separated due to mass evacuations and fathers going away to fight in wars. By the time the World War came to an end, Londoners had learned to live with uncertainty and hardship.

The conditions before the Blitz were hostile. Britain was recovering from the losses of the First World War. In fact, they had done pretty well in it. The construction of new houses was a prominent part of the British economy in the 1930s. Peace was returning to Britain, but the timeline wanted something else. Hitler rose to power and started World War II by invading Poland. Many countries suffered through the era of Hitler; Britain was not an exception to this. People spent those six years living in terror and anxiety. At any given point, Nazis could come and bomb their cities.

Before the Blitz happened, Britain and its population had to go through two forbidding events; the "Phoney Wars" and the "Battle of Britain." The mass evacuations, anticipated bombings, and other stressing events had the public in their depressing grasp. In the 1930s, Nazism grew to power with Hitler as their head. This rapid rise was a threat to peace in the European countries. Britain sensed that a war might happen soon; hence they started preparing for it. Many feared that air raids and gas attacks would be launched against the civilians. Thus, detailed plans were laid out for the Air Raid Precautions (ARP) department.

During the 1938 Munich Crisis, war seemed inevitable. This prompted the British government to implement preventive measures. Air raid shelters were distributed among the civilians, night-time blackouts were planned, and approx 38 million gas masks were issued. Arrangements were also made for the mass evacuations of children that were about to happen in Britain. The plan was to migrate the urban children into safer regions like rural areas. At this time, Britain also became home to 4,000 *Ninos*, children who got caught up in the fight against fascism in Spain. Just months before World War II started, 10,000 Jewish children from Germany, Austria, and Czechoslovakia were sent by their parents to Britain on Kinder transport. This was their attempt to save their children from Nazi persecution (IWM, 2018a).

On September 1, 1939, World War II was declared with the German invasion of Poland. As soon as the British government got the news, mass evacuations of children started from cities and towns. This was the most significant and gigantic internal migration Britain had ever seen. Most children migrated through trains with their schools and lived with foster parents. The evacuation was like an adventure for some because they had never seen the countryside before. As for the others, they felt homesick and unhappy. Foster parents were often left shocked by the poor hygiene and diets of the children living in the inner city. Equally, some town children found themselves living in primitive and isolated farming communities that did not have access to electricity or running water.

This early period of evacuations and terror came to be known as the "Phoney War." The expected air raids never happened, making many people feel casual about their safety. Due to this, many evacuees went to their homes. But we all know how history played after that. Nazis invaded France and forced them to surrender. Air raids began in the cities of Britain, leading to another wave of evacuations. Thousands of children were vacated and sent to foreign countries like North America, Australia, New Zealand, and South Africa.

After the fall of France in 1940, fear invaded people's minds. The fear of the German invasion of Great Britain. The Channel Islands got occupied in early July by the Nazis. People were terrified as Britain was on the brink of getting occupied by them. Shortly afterward, Nazis started chains of air raids against Britain. It was believed that the Families in southern and eastern England were on the front lines of the attacks. More children were evacuated to safer places, often from the regions where they had previously been relocated. The people left became the spectators of the aerial dog fight between Britain's Royals Air Force and German bombers during the Battle of Britain.

Boys of age 17 and above joined the home guards to help defend villages and towns from the anticipated enemy invasion. The Austrians and Germans that lived in Britain now faced the risk of internment. Around 14,000 Austrian and German people, including 500 children, were confined on the Isle of Man as the "enemy aliens" (IWM, 2018a).

The Blitz started on the "Black Saturday" of September 7, 1940. Many German bombers entered the city of London with a single goal; to plant the seed of terror in Britain. The period during the Blitz was horrifying. People had to find refuges to protect themselves from the bombing and the debris which followed it. Many used Anderson and Morrison shelters for safety, but for those who didn't have access to them, London Tube stations were the only option left. These Tube shelters protected at least 1,00,000 to 1,50,000 people on any given night (Gershon, 2018).

During the initial months of the Blitz, London was attacked for 57 consecutive nights. There was not a single night where the Londoners could sleep without feeling anxious. Later on, hundreds of tons of bombs were dropped on the major cities and ports on numerous occasions. The Blitz had killed over 7,736 children, and around 7,622 got impaired for their whole lives. Many of them became orphans as they lost their family members. Even after suffering a lot, many children were involved in relief efforts. Those over 16, the Girl guides and the Boy scouts, helped with the Air Raid Precautions (ARP) services. Children became the saviors of Britain during their hardships as they worked during the air raids, worked as messengers—fire watchers, and did voluntary services.

This work of helping people put the lives of children at significant risk. Many were killed on duty because of the constant bombings and air raids. Even after the Blitz ended, bombing continued till the termination of the world war. New weapons like the V1 flying bomb and V2 rocket were discovered in 1944 that caused enormous destruction and casualties.

As far as wartime houses are concerned, they range from dilapidated tenement slums to stately homes. Numerous residences still didn't have proper bathrooms and had outside lavatories. Children often shared beds with their brothers and sisters or parents, which was not a big deal. The homes were installed with the Morrison shelters as they were specifically designed to keep people safe from bombings. It was constructed from heavy steel and had enough space for two or three people to sleep at night. Although not everyone had access to these shelters, forcing them to look for a safe place.

During the war, over 200,000 houses were destroyed by the bombs. Children had to relocate numerous times, often into prefabricated, emergency homes. In total, around 34 million address changes took place during the war. The war made people suffer through shortages of food and clothing. People living on the front lines of Britain had to suffer a lot due to them being the primary targets of the enemy. The imported food could no longer reach Britain in large quantities, increasing the hardships. Hence, to cope with the situation, the British government introduced food rationing in January 1940.

Meat, sugar, fish, butter, cheese, and eggs were rationed due to their short supply. People were encouraged to grow their own food under the government's "Dig for Victory" campaign. Every available plot was used for farming to maximize food production. Kensington Gardens was also utilized to grow cabbages instead of flowers. Child health and welfare was the top priority of the British government, so children and expecting mothers got special allotments of milk. Vitamins were provided to them in the form of oranges and cod liver.

From June 1941, even the clothes became rationed. Clothing coupon books were issued by the government to all the Londoners. Adults were allowed to use 66 coupons per year. On the other side, growing children were given additional coupons as their clothes would get small after a particular time. Parents were also allowed to exchange the clothes and shoes that their children had outgrown with large items from the clothing exchanges. A pair of shoes would cost a person seven coupons; buying a coat would mean a loss of 16 coupons (Harvey, 2016). The books had pages of different colors, and a person was permitted to use only one color at a time. The government announced whenever the next color could be used. This measure was essential as it prevented people from using all their coupons quickly.

The schoolings of children were heavily disrupted during the Blitz and World War II. Mass evacuations of 1939 heavily upset the education system for months. Although the children were evacuated with their schoolmates and teachers, the books and stationaries were not enough for everyone to use. Over 2,000 schools were requisitioned by the military for war use. One in five schools were completed destroyed or damaged, thanks to the German bombing. Air raids frequently stopped lessons for hours, which resulted in lesser attendance. Although most of the schools were evacuated, some decided to stay. They saw this as an opportunity and converted the cellars and basements into makeshift classrooms.

When the war began in 1939, most children left schools when they turned 14. To increase attendance in schools, the British government implemented the Education Act in 1944. This act introduced free secondary education for all children, and education was made compulsory till the age of 15. But it didn't take effect until after the end of the war.

Despite the wartime conditions and Blitz, children still had time for their games and entertainment. Some cinemas were opened during the Blitz, a popular site among teenagers and children. No matter how fierce a bomb site would look, it still could be used as play areas for children. They would hunt for the shrapnel souvenirs in the debris of cities. Toys and games played by the children often had wartime themes. Captain W. E. John's novels—*Biggles* and *Worrals of the Women's Auxiliary Air Force* would excite children as they told about the heroic exploits and wartime adventures. The arrival of a large number of American troops and airmen in 1942 led to an exciting development in the culture of Britain. How? They did it by bringing the American culture to British children for the first time. American servicemen were generous enough with their off-rationed chocolates and chewing gums as they organized children's parties and treats at their bases.

The ending of the Blitz happened on May 11. Nazis made sure that the end of the Blitz made an everlasting wound in people's minds. That day, more than 700 tons of bombs were dropped by the Luftwaffe, which killed around 1,500 Londoners. Most prominent buildings like the British Museum, the House of Commons, Westminster Abbey were severely damaged. People lost their loved ones, which made an everlasting wound in their lives. Their houses were destroyed. It is believed that one in six Londoners were made homeless at one point during the Blitz. Finally, the Blitz ended after 8 months, but now it was a challenging road. The Britishers needed to rebuild and recreate their homelands destroyed by the Nazis.

After the Blitz, the government tried ascertaining the total damage inflicted by the Nazis on them. It is estimated that around 100,000 houses were doomed only in the city of London. The total number of Britain accounted for millions. Over 80,000 Londoners were either killed by the bombs or were seriously injured. Just on May 10, 1941, more than 3,000 of them died due to the final wave of the Blitz. Bomb injuries suffered by the Londoners made it difficult for the authorities to identify wounded people. Hence, the government came up with the idea of identity tags. They encouraged the civilians to wear these identity tags to speed up the process of identification. Many Londoners wore metal bracelets on which their personal details were engraved. Identity bracelets were attached to a charm of Saint Christopher, the patron saint of safe travel. This would assure the wearers that they are going on a safe journey (Museum of London, n.d.).

The war ended in 1945 with the surrender of the Nazis and Japan. The Victory in Europe (VE Day) was celebrated on May 8. On VE day, thousands of street parties, fancy dress parades, and bonfires were held across Europe. Even though the food was rationed, great efforts were put into providing treats to children. Similar events took place on August 15, when Europe celebrated the surrender of Japan. After the war ended, family lives remained disrupted for months, sometimes even longer. Evacuees, who were first separated for years from their families, now returned to their homes. Fathers who returned from wars or the prisoner of war (POW) camps were unrecognizable for the children who never knew them. The people who lost their family members and loved ones during the war, their lives could never be the same again.

The Blitz had caused mass destruction in London and other cities. In 1939, when the war started, the government announced that it would pay postwar compensation for buildings, furniture, and clothing damaged by enemy action. In June 1940, the anticipation of air raids rose. Hence, the British government had to do something to reassure the population. So, they agreed to make advanced payments to the bombed families. Then, the Blitz started, and the losses were more than the expectations of the government. Thus, in March 1941, a new Wars Damage Act was created, which levied a compulsory annual premium on all property owners. It was backed by Treasury funding to provide contents and buildings insurance against bombing for every dwelling in the country. Although the payments were to be made in advance, the submission and verification of these claims took years.

While the war was being fought, rebuilding the country was impossible. The majority of the raw materials and production were directed towards military demands. Household goods and furniture were low in supply and expensive. The central and local authorities carried out more than 10 million building repairs, but the pace was slow. New house buildings, which were a significant part of the economy of the 1930s, ceased during the Blitz.

Overcrowding and the deterioration in living conditions were probably the most widely felt consequence of the Blitz. The mass destruction of the Blitz encouraged the government to create an elite urban plan, the plan which would recreate Britain (*The Cruel Cost of the Blitz*, 2017).

References

10 incredible stories of bravery during the Blitz. (n.d.). Imperial War Museums. https://www.iwm.org.uk/history/10-incredible-stories-of-bravery-during-the-blitz

Academic. (n.d.). *The Airmen's Stories – F/O G Ashfield.* The Battle of Britain London Monument. https://en-academic.com/dic.nsf/enwiki/70975

Aceto, G. (2009, November 23). *Shadows of the Blitz in today's London.* HistoryNet. https://www.historynet.com/shadows-of-the-blitz-in-todays-london/

Air warfare. (n.d.). Encyclopedia Britannica. https://www.britannica.com/topic/air-warfare#ref53045

Angus Calder. (1997). *Myth of the Blitz.* Pimlico.

Bamford, T. (2020, March 14). *Bombing Berlin: The biggest wartime raid on Hitler's capital.* The National WWII Museum | New Orleans. https://www.nationalww2museum.org/war/articles/bombing-berlin-biggest-wartime-raid-hitlers-capital

Britannica, T. Editors of Encyclopedia (2018). *The Blitz | World War II.* In Encyclopædia Britannica. https://www.britannica.com/event/the-Blitz

Evan and Evans. (2020, March 24). *[Guide] What was the Blitz 1940-41?* Evan Evans Tours. https://evanevanstours.com/blog/blitz-guide/

Every bomb dropped by the British & Americans during WW2. (2017, April 12). Brilliant Maps. https://brilliantmaps.com/uk-us-bombs-ww2/

Examples of bomb damage still seen today. (n.d.). World War Two Inert Air Dropped Ordance. http://www.ww2airdroppedordnance.com/bomb-damage.html

Field, G. (2002). Nights Underground in Darkest London: The Blitz, 1940-1941. *International Labor and Working-Class History*, 62, 11–49. https://www.jstor.org/stable/27672803?seq=4

Forgotten Stories. (2017, August 25). *Forgotten Stories: Black Saturday.* London's Royal Docks. https://londonsroyaldocks.com/forgotten-stories-black-saturday/

Francois, E. (2018, March 9). *When German trains saved Jewish kids.* Exberliner. https://www.exberliner.com/politics/when-german-trains-saved-jewish-kids/

Geary, P. J., Heather, P. J., Strauss, G., Sheehan, J. J., Berentsen, W. H., Turner, H. A., Schleunes, K. A., Kirby, G. H., Elkins, T. H., Leyser, K. J., Bayley, C. C., Hamerow, T. S., Duggan, L. G., Barkin, K., and Wallace-Hadrill, J. M. (2022, April 27). *Germany | Facts, geography, maps, & history.* In Encyclopædia Britannica. https://www.britannica.com/place/Germany

Gershon, L. (2018, August 20). *What life was like during the London Blitz.* Jstor Daily. https://daily.jstor.org/what-life-was-like-during-the-london-blitz/

Gershon, L. (2019, February 18). What Life Was Like During the London Blitz | JSTOR Daily. JSTOR Daily. https://daily.jstor.org/what-life-was-like-during-the-london-blitz/

Gilbert, M. (1991). *Churchill: a life*. Heinemann.

Gunther, J. (1919). Inside Europe. In *Internet Archive* (pp. 328, 332–333). The Haddon   Craftsmen.   https://archive.org/details/in.ernet.dli.2015.149663/page/n349/mode/2up?view=theater

Harvey, I. (2016, July 20). *Clothing rationing in Britain during WWII*. War History   Online.   https://www.warhistoryonline.com/featured/clothing-rationing-wwii.html?chrome=1&edg-c=1

Higginbotham, A. (2016, January 6). *There are still thousands of tons of unexploded bombs in Germany, left over from World War II*. Smithsonian Magazine; Smithsonian Magazine. https://www.smithsonianmag.com/history/seventy-years-world-war-two-thousands-tons-unexploded-bombs-germany-180957680/

Hooton, E. R., & Internet Archive. (1999). *Eagle in flames: the fall of the Luftwaffe*. In Internet Archive. London : Brockhampton. https://archive.org/details/eagleinflamesfal0000hoot

Imperial War Museums. (2018). *What you need to know about rationing in the Second World War*. Imperial War Museums. https://www.iwm.org.uk/history/what-you-need-to-know-about-rationing-in-the-second-world-war

Ingersoll, R. (1940). Report On England, November 1940. In *Internet Archive* (p. 127). University of Michigan. https://archive.org/details/ReportOnEngland/page/n145/mode/2up?view=theater

IWM. (2018a). *Growing up in the Second World War*. Imperial War Museums. https://www.iwm.org.uk/history/growing-up-in-the-second-world-war

IWM. (2018b). *How children's lives changed during the Second World War*. Imperial War Museums. https://www.iwm.org.uk/history/how-childrens-lives-changed-during-the-second-world-war

Jewsbury, M. (2010, September 5). *The Blitz: Survivors' stories*. The Independent. https://www.independent.co.uk/news/uk/this-britain/the-blitz-survivors-stories-2070845.html

Kindy, D. (2020, February 24). *How Winston Churchill endured the Blitz—and taught the people of England to do the same*. Smithsonian Magazine. https://www.smithsonianmag.com/history/how-winston-churchill-endured-blitzand-taught-people-england-do-same-180974229/

London Walking Tours. (n.d.). *The city in the Blitz walk - London At War*. London Walking Tours. https://www.london-walking-tours.co.uk/london-blitz-walk.htm

Mackay, R. (2003). *Heinkel He 111*. Crowood Press.

Manston Airfield, H. of. (2021, September 15). *Battle of Britain Day, 15th September 1940 – History of Manston Airfield*. History of Manston Airfield. https://www.manstonhistory.org.uk/battle-of-britain-day-15th-september-1940/

Murray, W. (1983). Strategy for defeat the Luftwaffe 1933 -1945. DTIC. https://apps.dtic.mil/sti/pdfs/ADA421966.pdf

Nambi, K. (2021, February 9). *Battle of Beams the technology war during World War II.* Medium. https://medium.com/lessons-from-history/battle-of-beams-the-technology-war-during-world-war-ii-a611a31454b

Net, F. (2021, February 10). *The deadly WW2 parachute mine: How 2,200lb German bombs devastated London in the Blitz.* Forces Network. https://www.forces.net/heritage/wwii/deadly-ww2-parachute-mine-how-2200lb-german-bombs-devastated-london-blitz

Overy, R. J., & Internet Archive. (2005). *The air war, 1939-1945.* In Internet Archive. Washington, D.C. : Potomac Books, Inc. https://archive.org/details/airwar193919450000over_n5j5

Overy, R. J., White, J., & Whitaker, G. (2016). *All About History–Book of the Battle of Britain.* Imagine Publishing.

Panter-Downes, M. (1940, September 21). *Living through the Blitz.* The New Yorker. https://www.newyorker.com/magazine/1940/09/21/living-through-the-blitz

Pensioners, C. (2020, October 9). *Inspiring stories of survival to mark 80 years since the Blitz.* Royal Hospital Chelsea. https://www.chelsea-pensioners.co.uk/news/inspiring-stories-survival-mark-80-years-blitz

Ray, J. (2000). *The night blitz : 1940-1941.* Cassell.

Ray, J. P., & Internet Archive. (2000). *The night blitz, 1940-1941.* In Internet Archive. London : Cassell. https://archive.org/details/night-blitz1940190000rayj_z4k2/page/n299/mode/2up

Richards, D. (n.d.). *HyperWar: Royal Air Force 1939–1945: Volume I: The Fight at Odds* [Chapter V]. IBiblio. https://www.ibiblio.org/hyperwar/UN/UK/UK-RAF-I/UK-RAF-I-5.html

Salisbury, H. (2012). *The War on Our Doorstep: How the Blitz Changed the East End Forever.* Ebury.

Shakespeare, N. (2018). *Six minutes in May: How Churchill unexpectedly became Prime Minister.* Vintage.

Talarico, J. (2018). *How the Luftwaffe fought the Battle Of Britain.* Imperial War Museums. https://www.iwm.org.uk/history/how-the-luftwaffe-fought-the-battle-of-britain

Taylor, J. (2018). *How Churchill led Britain to victory in the Second World War.* Imperial War Museums. https://www.iwm.org.uk/history/how-churchill-led-britain-to-victory-in-the-second-world-war

The cruel cost of the Blitz. (2017, December 1). HistoryExtra. https://www.historyextra.com/period/second-world-war/the-cruel-cost-of-the-blitz/

Trueman, C. N. (2022, April 28). *The impact of the Blitz on London.* History Learning Site. https://www.historylearningsite.co.uk/world-war-two/world-war-two-in-western-europe/britains-home-front-in-world-war-two/the-impact-of-the-blitz-on-london/

USAF, L. C. E. L. (n.d.). *HyperWar: The Battle of Britain--A German perspective.* IBiblio. https://www.ibiblio.org/hyperwar/ETO/BOB/BoB-German/index.html

White, I. (2007, May 30). *The History Of Air Intercept Radar The British Night-fighter 1935 1959.* Read Free Book. https://readsfree.com/book/the-history-of-air-intercept-radar-the-british-nightfighter-1935-1959/

White. (2016, August 16). *The first raid on London by the Luftwaffe.* Forces War Records. https://www.forces-war-records.co.uk/blog/2016/08/16/the-first-raid-on-london-by-the-luftwaffe

Wikipedia. (2020, March 9). *Bombing of Berlin in World War II.* Wikipedia. https://en.wikipedia.org/wiki/Bombing_of_Berlin_in_World_War_II

Wikipedia. (2022, March 25). *The Blitz.* Wikipedia. https://en.wikipedia.org/wiki/The_Blitz#cite_note-Cooper_1981

Wukovits, J. (2022, January 25). *A World War II survivor recalls the London Blitz.* British Heritage. https://britishheritage.com/history/world-war-ii-survivor-london-blitz

Your guide to the Blitz, plus 9 places affected by the bombings. (2020, September 7). HistoryExtra. https://www.historyextra.com/period/second-world-war/the-blitz-what-happened-how-many-died-blitz-meaning/

Zabecki, D. T. (2006, June 12). *How North Africa became a battleground in World War II.* Historynet. https://www.historynet.com/how-north-africa-became-a-battleground-in-world-war-ii/

Printed in Dunstable, United Kingdom